SAY THIS
NOT THAT
TO YOUR PROFESSOR

36 TALKING TIPS
FOR COLLEGE SUCCESS

Second Edition

By Ellen Bremen

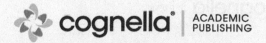

cognella® | ACADEMIC PUBLISHING

Bassim Hamadeh, CEO and Publisher
Michael Simpson, Vice President of Acquisitions
Jamie Giganti, Senior Managing Editor
Jess Busch, Senior Graphic Designer
Kristina Stolte, Acquisitions Editor
Michelle Piehl, Project Editor
Alexa Lucido, Licensing Coordinator
Joyce Lue, Interior Designer

Cover image copyright © 2011 iStockphoto LP/Dean Mitchell.

Printed in the United States of America

ISBN: 978-1-5165-0498-5 (pbk) / 978-1-5165-0499-2 (br)

Praise for the previous edition

Advance Praise

"Ellen Bremen's book will help students avoid worst-case scenarios in the classroom and on their transcripts, with concrete tools and strategies for communicating effectively with professors. Students will develop skills for college and for life."

— Jennifer Worick, The New York Times bestselling co-author of *The Worst-Case Scenario Survival Handbook: College*

"The content is wide-ranging. The voice Is conversational and inviting. The advice is specific, clear, and practical—just the sort of information that's likely to help students be more successful in college. I wish I'd known more of this when I was an undergraduate."

— Ron Adler, professor Santa Barbara City College and author of *Understanding Human Communication*

"Ellen has amazing wisdom about the inner workings of college. She is the Dear Abby of college professors, such a respectful and open author."

— Vicki Davis, co-founder of Flat Classroom Projects and author of the award-winning Cool Cat Teacher blog

"*Say This NOT That to Your Professor* gives students the words to say to build a bridge and create the kind of life-changing, student-professor relationships college success is all about. Ellen shows students how to make the most of these relationships to fuel their educational goals. This book is a must-read for every college student."

— Isa Adney, author of *Community College Success: How to Finish with Friends, Scholarships, Internships, and the Career of Your Dreams*

"Getting into college is only the beginning. What really counts is squeezing the very most out of your time at college. Ellen Bremen does an excellent job of sharing what it takes to not only survive in college, but more importantly, how to communicate to succeed."

—Lynn O'Shaughnessy, higher-ed expert for CBS MoneyWatch, consulting director of college planning at University of California, San Diego Extension,and author of *The College Solution*, an Amazon best seller

Praise from Ellen's Students and Blog Readers

"Students in Ellen Bremen's class are rewarded with a knowledgeable and truly modern-day professor. She guides her students through the nuances of interpersonal communication, reaching them through her progressive teaching style. Whether teaching her students how to communicate with their professor or how not to express anger, Ellen Bremen inspires learning."

— Spencer Wright

"The information and tools I learned in Ellen Bremen's class, gave me insight into my own thinking and communication style, insight into other styles, and, I believe, helped me become a better communicator. Instead of simply gaining information, her course helped me grow as a person."

— Tisha Gramann

"After Ellen Bremen's class, I felt empowered to step up to the plate and challenge myself. Ellen gives people a voice that is truly amazing!"

—Anthony Endsley

"Ellen Bremen showed me how not just to talk about myself, but how to believe in myself. I am currently empowering myself with an education that will provide me the opportunity of doing what I am capable of instead of just doing what takes the least effort."

— Teresa Covert

"I used your 'I' grade advice today. Thank you! I finished with an A, two B's, and an I."

— Erin Breedlove (student reader from the Chatty Professor blog)

"I feel much better. If I needed to speak with a department chair again, I could without feeling terribly nervous."

—(student reader from the Chatty Professor blog; name withheld)

"I recently asked a professor (early!) what I could do to achieve a 4.0 in his class. He explained his grading system. I turned in my papers early and then made his suggested changes. I aced each assignment. I would not have thought to use Professor Bremen's ideas had I not read her book!"

— Don Crawley, student and author of *The Compassionate Geek: Mastering Customer Service for IT Professionals*

CONTENTS

Grades

Managing Assignments/Your Schedule

Dealing with Technology

Building a Relationship with Your Professor/ Other Campus Resources

SECTION 2: CLASS ISSUES YOUR PROFESSOR WON'T DISCUSS—AND MAY NOT WANT YOU TO KNOW

Acknowledgments

An author writes a book, and a village upholds the author of that book. Here's who rallied around me:

Sherri Patterson and **Cheryl Colehour**: Sherri was my best friend for twelve years. We planned to return to college together and earn our degrees when we were "older" students. She never got that chance. Sherri died of breast cancer in October 2000. I would have never gone back to school to study communication if not for her, and hence this book wouldn't exist.

Cheryl was my new friend in 2010. She, too, had been diagnosed with breast cancer and, while on hiatus from her work in instructional design, was clamoring for work to do during treatment. Her masterful touch editing the first edition of this book led to my landing an agent and, ultimately, a publisher. Cheryl died in November 2011.

My husband, **Mark**, and my two children, **Brenna** and **Scott.** With love and immense appreciation for supporting me through both editions of this book.

To **every single student** whose academic journey I've had the privilege of sharing for a moment in time.

To my **colleagues**, past and present, who strengthened me with their excellence at Highline College.

To **Simone Rico**, for reasons she'll know.

To those who provided the foundation for my own degrees, both in Postsecondary Education (**Dr. Cliff McClain, Dr. Paul Meacham, Dr. Rosemarie Deering**), and in Communication (**Dr. Thomas Burkholder, Dr. Beth DeLisle, Dr. Erika Engstrom**). I carry and use your teachings every single day in my work with students.

To my editor, **Michelle Piehl**, acquisitions editor, **Kristina Stolte**, and the entire team at Cognella. Thank you for taking this book on a new journey!

To the industry professionals who contributed to this edition, I value you! Your wisdom seamlessly bridged these scenarios for the workplace—a gift for every student: **Mark Babbitt, Angelee Bailey, Mark Bremen, Kelsi Burkhart, Marianne Carreno, Susan Carroll, Ted Carroll, Elouise Cassatt, Don Crawley, Sharon Cupp, Jonathan Davidson, Jennifer Dempsey, Teresa Fernandes, Eric Garay, Stephen Jablonsky, Dave Kerpen, Liz Kislik, Hazel Lorrin, Steve Levy, Kristin MacIntosh, Shawn Murphy, Ted Rubin, Nicolette Shea, Dawn Rasmussen, Donna Svei, Judith Turney, Connie Wiatrak.**

And, finally, I want to acknowledge every student who will risk and ultimately triumph from having the courage to Find. Your. Voice. and use it!

Introduction

Welcome to Say This, NOT That to Your Professor! *This introduction is organized in the same format you'll find throughout the book. The Real Story will give you a true story* about the scenario you may encounter. The Backstory will offer you behind-the-scenes insight on that situation, then tips on how to deal with it.*

Let's start with the real story of why this book was written.

The Real Story

Nicole, a student advisee, sat in my office, firing off complaints about her professor. She couldn't follow what was happening in her class and hadn't talked to the professor about it.

"I don't know what to say to him," Nicole said.

I replied, "The professor can't help you if she doesn't know you're struggling."

Nicole shot back, "I'm going to fail! I just know it!"

"You don't have to fail. Go talk to the prof!" I prodded.

"She doesn't care. If she did, she'd check in with me. My grades haven't exactly been good!"

"Seriously, Nicole," I said, looking right into her eyes. "What's your role in your education? Your professor probably isn't going to come to you. She expects that you'll tell her if you're struggling."

Nicole didn't say anything further.

You might think I was being confrontational, but Nicole and I had a great relationship. She had actually been my student for a few classes, and I knew I could speak to her straight.

When Nicole left my office that day, we hadn't really gotten anywhere. *I* made a mistake, not in my directness with Nicole, but in not coaching her through the exact words to say to the professor. I was fairly new to teaching; it was only my second year. I should have realized that telling someone what they should say is much different than suggesting the words they can use to say it.

I knew that Nicole could easily fall through the cracks because she wouldn't go to her professor. This happens to students every single day in colleges all over the place. They suffer in silence, then GPAs fall apart. They may skip class or drop out. Students feel helpless and hopeless, and professors figure that another student fell off the face of the earth or simply couldn't hack it.

After my meeting with Nicole, I started to notice other times when students couldn't or wouldn't self-advocate or handle situations properly. Sometimes, I couldn't believe things that students *would* say, not realizing that they risked the perception of their work ethic—or they just sounded clueless and full of excuses. I considered how much this type of communication could ultimately hurt students in the workplace. After all, could *I* say some of these things to my superiors and keep my job? No! The more years I taught, the more the examples mounted. I actually kept a list of them on a legal pad in my desk drawer.

During this time (and I'm really going to date myself, even though I'm only in my midforties), societal communication was changing as well. Fewer students connected with each other between classes. Instead, they were buried in their devices. Why talk when you can IM, text, etc.? But communication in college rarely happens that way. Instead, conversations and interactions occur mostly face to face or via e-mail. So between students saying the wrong thing and saying nothing at all, they were losing precious opportunities to practice critical communication skills.

I had another epiphany: professors felt frustrated about student interactions, but most would never tell students. Professors complain to each other ("Can you believe she said ... ?") in person and *definitely* on social media, but we wouldn't tell students what they were doing wrong or how to interact more effectively. Talk about a communication gap!

The Backstory

Now you have it: why I wrote this book.

There are tons of college success guides on the market, but not one solely deals with the relationship between the two people who interact in college every single day: you and your professor.

Most students don't think about this when they think about college. You probably fretted about how you'd survive Organic Chem and Calculus in one term, how you'd afford $500 for textbooks, or how you'd fare with the campus social scene.

But did you ever once think about what you'd say when:
You're going to be absent?
You turn in a late paper?
You need help?
You don't understand why you got a C instead of an A, and you're mad?

Probably not. And you aren't alone. Students who ace classes and those who are struggling don't know what to say either. Then they may say the wrong thing.

Professors become annoyed and wonder why students can't interact in a professional way. You become annoyed and you feel misunderstood. Worst of all, your grade may be suffering!

Your professor will very likely help you solve your academic problem, but if you interact in an unproductive or unprofessional way, your professor might not correct you and tell you how you could have come across in a clear, confident, and competent way. This is the instruction you must master for the workplace. It could mean the difference between getting, keeping, and moving up in a career.

The tips in this book can change all that. You are going to deal with your professors every day that you are in college, and I'm ready to help you start talking! I want you to have inside tips on how to interact so your professors will respond in a positive manner and you'll feel solid in your communication skills.

Try to view every conversation with your professor, including the difficult ones, as workplace practice. By learning to use your voice in a professional way, you'll build necessary skills for your career. And you can even use the discussions as examples for interviews or promotions.

Ready to go for it? Are you ready to create opportunities rather than excuses? Are you ready to properly stand up for yourself when you're concerned about classes, grades, or anything else college-related? Are you ready to have improved relationships with your professors, the benefits and mentorship that can come from experiencing their knowledge, and most of all, better grades?

Of course you are, so let's talk about what to do next!

How to Use This Guide

Say This, NOT That to Your Professor is meant to be a "throughout your college career"-type of text. Keep it with you at all times, either in hard copy or on a digital device. You never know when a situation might arise, and you want to have the words ready when you need them.

Now that you have this book, take a look at the Table of Contents. You may not have experienced the scenarios such as absences, late work, or getting a letter of recommendation yet, but you likely will. Familiarize yourself with the topics; that way, you can go right to that chapter. You do not need to read this chapter from start to finish. Reference the subjects as you need them.

Here is how you will use the sections in this book:

The Real Story

Examples of actual students who've faced a similar situation and how they handled, or mishandled, it.

The Backstory

A rare glimpse inside a professor's mind. You'll learn what a professor really thinks about the way students speak or behave in that situation. You'll also find out about college policies and class procedures so you'll know how to navigate them. Finally, you'll learn how the right words can empower you.

The next sections move you into the actual verbal tips:

Ask Yourself This *and* Think This, Not That

In these two sections, you'll evaluate current communication patterns and work toward changing unproductive thoughts you may have about your situation.

Say This

An actual script to practice or paraphrase in your own words before meeting with a professor to resolve your issue.

The words I'm giving you are professional and proactive. Use these phrases to solve issues with clarity and confidence. You'll have a far greater chance of achieving the outcomes you want. This early practice with your professor will help prepare you for similar interactions with supervisors, colleagues, and even in your personal life. Isn't that awesome?

Not That

You'll find out what ineffective, clueless statements you'll want to avoid—ones that are said by many students who don't realize how their words are coming across.

The End Note

Each chapter will conclude with an additional tip or two or an overview about the situation.

The Career Note NEW!

This new edition of *Say This, NOT That* will provide you with an industry perspective for each situation you may encounter in college. Professionals from various industries will give you back-story on their experiences. You'll have a real-world perspective to inspire and motivate you to use college as training for your professional life.

Before I close, just so you know, the term *professor* interchangeably refers to all educators, instructors, facilitators, lecturers, adjuncts, teachers, etc. If someone is teaching you, the advice I'm offering will likely fit.

Are you ready to give yourself an amazing class and college experience?

Are you ready to find your voice?

Let's begin the conversation!

Names and particular details of all situations have been modified to protect student privacy.

A special note about depression/anxiety

If you are one of the millions of people who suffer with depression and/or anxiety, you are not alone. Aside from grade issues, "Should I tell my professor about my depression/anxiety?" is one of the most commonly asked question.

While I realize you may feel embarrassed, uncomfortable, and fearful about sharing this information, I want you to think about the potential ramifications if you don't. Students have expressed being so paralyzed by their emotional state that they couldn't get out of the car to come to class. Some students with depression/anxiety sit out in the parking lot, willing themselves to make a move, but they simply can't. Others are at home, feeling the same way.

Your professor is one part of an entire campus team that can support you with depression or any other challenges you're facing. Confide in your professor if you struggle with these issues. Say, "This feels hard for me to talk about, but I want to share that I am currently struggling with anxiety (or whatever). I do not want this to get in my way this term."

With this conversation, your professor can lead you to other campus services such as counseling and even disability services (if you have medical documentation, then emotional/mental illness definitely qualifies for accommodations). Then you'll have a team on your side to help you get through difficult moments where you are trying to "do school" and manage depression, anxiety, etc.

The worst thing you can do is isolate yourself. As someone who has faced a decades-long struggle to manage anxiety/depression, I know firsthand that one large or small failure or disappointment can send things into overdrive. What's even worse is that most sufferers are well aware of their self-sabotage but just can't get out of their own way.

I have had hundreds of students over the years who sought out counseling or other resources and then were able to successfully get through their term. I'm not saying that the outcome was all As. I'm not saying there weren't bumps. But the vicious cycle of feelings, then inaction, then worse feelings, were managed in a different way by having others' help on board.

Share your struggles. Get yourself a team. You deserve it.

SECTION 1

Class Issues Your Professor Won't Discuss With You (But Wishes Someone Would).

- Parents

- Classroom/Peers

- Grades

- Managing Assignments/Your Schedule

- Dealing with Technology

- Building a Relationship with Your Professor/Other Campus Resources

Parents

1. ■ Parents Handling Your Problems

What You Might Think:

Mom talked to my teachers in high school when I had problems. I'll let her continue doing her good work.

What Your Professor Thinks:

Your parents have no business taking care of your business in college.

The Real Story

"My professor writes nasty feedback on my papers. It feels like he's attacking me!"

Beck, one of my advisees, sat in my office, angry at his professor and even more freaked out that he might not make it through his class.

"What kinds of things does he say?" I asked.

"Things like, 'Did you *not* understand this source wasn't credible?'"

I could hardly blame Beck for his reaction. Who would want feedback with that kind of tone?

"I want to drop that class!" Beck said, hitting about a five in volume—noteworthy for a typically quiet guy.

If Beck withdrew, he would not receive a refund. It was already midterm. And let's be real: we can't just run away from difficult people. Unfortunately, they are everywhere.

"Why not talk to the professor? Schedule a meeting and discuss what's bothering you," I suggested.

Beck looked at me like he'd rather have surgery without anesthesia.

"You can say, 'Professor, I appreciate your thoughts about my work, but I'm struggling with your written comments. They sound very critical of me as a person, rather than the writing. I'm nervous about turning other work in. Can I have some specific instructions on how to improve?'"

"I can't do that," Beck muttered. "I don't like arguments."

"Listen," I said. "You have to tell your professor you aren't comfortable. You deserve feedback that makes sense and doesn't make you feel this way. Think about when you're dealing with a boss. If your boss is always nasty to you, you'd figure out how to deal with it so you could do a good job, right? This professor may not realize how his comments are coming across."

Beck reluctantly agreed to make an appointment with the professor and then follow up with me. However, Beck didn't show up to his professor's office.

His mother did.

First, she called me. "Mrs. Bremen, Beck is having big trouble with one of his professors," she snapped. "This guy is treating

Beck like he doesn't do anything right! I need to see this jerk and find out why he's putting down my kid."

"I'm sorry," I said. "Legally, I can't discuss this situation with you."

"What do you mean?" she growled. "That's crazy. I am paying good money for this education. I have a right to know what's going on with my kid!"

The Backstory

Are you surprised that I used the word "legally"? I'm not a lawyer, nor do I play one on TV or Netflix. But I do know about the Family Educational Rights and Privacy Act of 1974 (FERPA), a law enabling students to keep their education a private matter once they hit age eighteen.

Legally, your professors can't discuss anything you're doing in college with your parents without your permission. The only exception to this law is if you sign paperwork with the registrar's office giving Mom and Dad freedom to see your educational records or speak to your professors.

Throwing a party in your head right now? Think this law is a *great* idea? It is! But only if you're willing to undertake the responsibility that the FERPA law gives you. In college, you are your own voice. You take care of your own business.

I realize this may be a shift for you. It's a shift for your parents, too. If Beck's mother called his teacher every time his pencil broke, suddenly "letting" him take care of his college-related affairs won't be an easy transition. I get it: my kids are twelve and seven, and except for the fact that I work at a college, I can't imagine the day that parent-teacher or student-led conferences—and full access to my children's educational records—end!

Yet I would want to know that I'm not wasting my money on my kids' college education. I would want to know if my daughter or son is snoozing in bed rather than sitting (or sleeping!) in class. I would also want to know if my kids are struggling. Once they get into college, though, it's technically (and legally) not my affair.

Putting my professor cap back on, here's my take: at school, I want you to have confidence to drive your education and your communication with professors. At home, I want you to keep your parents on your academic team. You're going to need their support as you are having these important conversations at school and advocating for yourself.

Ask Yourself This:

Did another adult handle issues for me in high school? Did they do this because I wanted them to? How did their intervention make me feel? Relieved? Thankful? Irresponsible? Incapable?

Did I ever go to teachers to solve my own problems? What was the best experience I had doing this? The worst?

How did I feel taking care of a problem myself? Confident? Motivated? If the situation didn't resolve in my favor, how important is that situation now that I'm in college?

Think This:

If I'm used to my parents handling things for me in high school, I'll get used to handling things myself.

If I'm already doing that, then I know I can do it in college.

It is totally understandable that you may not want to deal with your professors. Just remember, this isn't a job. You won't get fired if your professor doesn't like what you have to say. Handle yourself professionally and appropriately (which is why you're reading this book!) and you won't get kicked out, you won't fail, and your professor won't bite you. If the situation doesn't resolve, you have the option of talking to people who are higher up.

Not That:

I'm going to drop this class because I can't stand this professor!

You may choose to drop a class here or there, but you don't want to make it a regular habit. Dropping classes can throw off your graduation timeline, and it's expensive, depending on when you withdraw. And what if you don't like the next professor? Will you drop the next class, too? You'll learn far more by staying in a challenging situation and overcoming it than by running away. Give yourself the chance to gain that experience and the confidence that you'll feel from getting through it.

I'm going to sign the damned FER-whatever paper so my parents can tell that guy off!

Come on! This is college, and you are an adult! Fight your own battles. Your parents don't step into your arguments with your boyfriend, girlfriend, or best friend, do they? Believe in yourself. Use your good words to represent yourself. Regardless of the outcome, you'll gain skills every time you try.

Say This:

Do what Beck should have done—make an appointment with the professor and say:

> Thank you for seeing me today, Professor Frodo. When I read the comments you make on my papers, I feel like you are attacking my work. I am having a hard time focusing on improvement when the comments seem so harsh. Can I have specific feedback about my work so I can improve?

Use this strategy to deal with any other issue where you feel like the professor is talking down to you. Hopefully, you'll rarely, if ever, have to deal with something like this. But sometimes an unintended tone comes out, or the professor may just have a personality that doesn't click with yours. You may feel like the professor doesn't like you (and don't ask them if they do).

The truth is that your professor doesn't have to like you. You don't have to like them either. "Like" is a bonus in the student–professor relationship, and more often than not, you'll probably have it. But the only relationship you need with your professor is one of fairness in instruction and grading. If you don't get that, you can also say:

> I'm sensing that you are frustrated with me or my work. I want to do my best in this class. Can you give me specific advice about something I should be doing differently to improve what I'm turning in?

You must not like me very much.

I must be a total screwup. I can't do anything right in this class.

You're a real jerk. You don't care about your students' feelings.

Acting angry or like a victim will not get your message across. Instead, ask questions, use "I" language, and focus on getting the feedback that you need and deserve.

The End Note

Wondering what happened with Beck? He missed a huge opportunity to advocate for himself. When he allowed his mother to step in after our conversation, I wondered at what point he would take responsibility for his education and forge these critical working relationships with his professors.

I'll share another angle on a similar situation: Mary was a struggling student of mine. She skipped class, didn't follow through on assignments or studying, and she repeatedly fell apart on promises to her parents that she would do better.

Mary did sign FERPA paperwork giving her parents access to her educational records, but it didn't seem to matter. The only benefit Mary's parents had was that they could find out directly how poorly Mary was doing. Not surprisingly, Mary ended up on academic probation several times, ultimately requiring a hearing.

Unlike Beck, Mary did not opt to have her parents attend the hearing. I wasn't expecting her rationale, either: "If my parents came, I wouldn't take it seriously. I needed this to happen and I needed to go on my own." Mary ultimately turned things around for herself. Independence at that academic hearing was a clear first step.

Follow Mary's lead. If you do, you'll likely have a more productive relationship with your professors, you'll know what your professor expects from you (superimportant for your success!), and you'll start to believe in yourself that you can handle conflicts. This is a good thing, because conflict is everywhere.

Bottom line: college has no PTA. You've joined the SPA: the Student–Professor Association.

You hold the meetings.

You set the agendas.

You gain the academic and personal benefits that last you a lifetime.

The Career Note

A 2012 study cited in the *Wall Street Journal* stated that 11 percent of college graduates involve their parents in the interviewing process.[1] Here's an interviewer's take on this practice:

> *I had one mother contact me. I politely told her to have her son call to discuss the position, that I wouldn't discuss anything with her. She was a little surprised when I told her I hadn't received his resume. He had told her he already applied for the position. The woman's son called me about two hours later.*

---

1   http://www.wsj.com/articles/SB10001424127887323864604579066964214209866

I certainly did not have very high expectations for the candidate, but I was interested in him since we were desperately trying to find someone for that particular position. He interviewed well on the phone so I called her in for a panel interview. But, really, students show that they are responsible if they seek out and apply for a position on their own.

Theresa, healthcare

2. Talking to Parents about Failure

What You Might Think:

I can't tell my parents that I failed this term. They'll go crazy (kick me out of the house, think I'm a failure in life, cry, scream at me, etc.).

What Your Professor Thinks:

You need people who care about you on your academic team. Talk to them.

What Your Parent/Concerned Person Thinks:

I may be extremely angry, disappointed, devastated, etc., but ultimately, I care and I want to know what's going on with you so we can figure it out.

The Real Story

> "I messed up. My parents want to see my grades, and I can't let them. I failed, and I'm not living up to their expectations. I tried. What can I say to not make them more mad at me? I hate feeling like a failure to them."

> "I've been dangerously depressed, and I just let myself fail an entire quarter's worth of classes. I didn't understand the impact it would have on my financial aid and tried not to think about how it would affect my GPA. I might have to pay back my loans, and I may have lost them for good. I can't tell my parents about this. They will be devastated."

I wish e-mails like these were fake, but they aren't. They are from real students terrified to disclose their academic standing to their families. Students fear hurting, disappointing, or causing financial harm to whomever is supporting their education (parents, guardians, grandparents, or other interested parties).

I don't need to add more "Real Story" here. The painful e-mails speak for themselves. Let's jump into solutions.

The Backstory

Let me start by saying that I am a parent. Both my kids struggle in school. I could very well be in your parents' shoes one day:

my own kids might be afraid to tell me about their grades. So let's just say that I am sensitive to this situation from both sides.

That said, in the last chapter I told you that your parents shouldn't be doing school business for you. I meant that. But remember when I said that you still need your parents behind the scenes on your academic *team*? I meant that, too!

In the e-mail examples, the word "fail" came up several times. Quite often, the habits that lead to failure become a pattern: too little studying, too much socializing and procrastination, too little help in enough time for it to, well, help.

Parents go nuts seeing their kids repeat mistakes. Therefore, if you fear that your parents will go off on you for poor grades, they may feel frustrated about unproductive habits working against you. Their anger likely also stems from feeling helpless. Really, motivation, effort, time management, and self-advocacy are ultimately up to you. Your parents can make recommendations, but they can't put the work ethic into you.

You might be thinking, "But my bad grades aren't my fault. The professor was (insert: too boring, too strict, too *whatever*)." This may be true, but from your parents' perspective, they expect that *you* will take care of issues with your professor—or seek their guidance (or someone's guidance) to do so.

Because your parents know you and your habits—for better or worse—your communication strategy must reveal a proactive, immediate plan for tangible change. So, *before* you confront your parents to deliver bad news, not to mention steel yourself for "the lecture" that you'll get and may deserve, take these "pre-steps" to change the conversation:

First, talk to current professors about your grades. Send an e-mail to set an appointment and save a copy of the e-mail (I'll explain why in a moment).

Later chapters in this book will give you the words for those specific grade conversations. Your main goals are to come clean about your grades with the folks from whom you are earning them and to receive answers about how those grades happened.

Say that you know you've failed or that you are failing and discuss how you contributed to the failure ("I should have come to you sooner" is a good catch-all statement if you feel that the problem wasn't necessarily on your end). Make it clear that you want to change the outcome for the rest of the term, or for next term.

After speaking with the professor, visit your school's counseling office. You need more people on your academic team. Failure is incredibly stressful. Your college's counseling office can support you with issues that may be hindering your success. Grab a pamphlet from the counseling office and keep that with you.

Finally, figure out what other resources you can use at your college to change the outcome for next time: tutoring center, writing center, librarian support—anything.

Once you've done these things, and only after you've done them, then it's time to talk to your parents. Many students know that their parents have heard it all before, and part of the fear is that anything they say won't be believed anyway. This is why you have to show that you've taken concrete steps to create change. You've done this by expanding your support team and speaking to the prof to hatch a new plan.

I genuinely believe if you show your parents a different approach to solve the problem, they will see a different side of you and may become less upset. The key is that you actually have to follow through on the conversations you have. You don't want to lose your parents' trust further by saying you'll keep working with your prof or the counseling center, tutoring center, etc., and then not doing it.

Ask Yourself This:

What is the worst that will happen if I am honest with my parents about my struggles? Even if they are upset, would my parents rather know what's going on than be kept in the dark? What will happen if I keep this information from them for a long time and they find out?

Think This:

By creating a plan and using my support systems, on and off campus, I can turn this situation around. If I'm honest with my parents and honest with myself, I have a chance to do things differently.

Not That:

My parents will hate me because I've failed and I won't ever be able to recover.

Failure in college *is* recoverable. Even if you lose financial aid and have to take out a loan or find a way to pay for school, the situation can turn around. I'm not saying alternate paths will be easy, but they are possible. And, once your parents see that you're taking new steps, you'll earn their trust that you are serious about school.

Say This (to your parents):

I failed this term. My grades are not up to my own standards, and I'm sure you are going to be upset about them, too. I don't want to keep going like this. So here's what I've done to help the situation: I've talked to my professors (show your parents the e-mail) and from that conversation, I made _____ plan. I talked to the counseling center (show your parents the pamphlet) to figure out why I'm doing some of the things I'm doing. I am going to keep checking in with him/her every other week (once a month—whatever). I also realized that I could use some additional help in (math, English, etc.) and I looked into _____ (tutoring center, etc.). I am being proactive now about my grades, and I hope you will also help me by _____ (figure out some specific ways you can stay accountable to your parents to raise your grades). I realize you may want to yell at me or lecture me, but believe me, I've beat myself up over this already and I don't want to feel like this anymore. So now hopefully I have some help in place and I can change things.

Not That:

Crickets

Keeping information from your parents or others who care about you is the worst thing you can do. First, the secret will eat up your insides. Nervous stomachaches won't solve the problem. And your parents may find out anyway. Take control of the situation. Remember, your parents may flip out, but with a new strategy, you'll have a plan to move forward.

The End Note

As of this writing, my daughter is almost thirteen and in seventh grade. In fifth grade, she came home with a bad report card.

My husband and I probably feel like your family members: we do everything we can to help our daughter succeed, but one thing we can't do is put motivation inside of her.

You may not think our situation is like yours because my daughter is young. I'll tell you this: I was tempted to yell and lecture. Remember when I talked about that helpless feeling? I was totally there, and the helplessness increased my anger. Yet in my heart I knew that yelling might release tension (mine!), but it wouldn't cause her to create permanent change.

Instead, I asked my daughter how *she* felt about her grades. She felt horrible. She had already beaten herself up and knew that her dad and I would be disappointed. I sat in front of her while she curled up in an overstuffed chair and sobbed. She didn't cry because I yelled, but because of her disappointment in herself. I asked if she could label how she felt at that moment.

She replied, "Mad and embarrassed that I did so badly."

"Do you want to feel this way again?" I asked.

"No, of course not!"

"Well, what can you do to make sure you don't feel this way again?"

My daughter wiped her face and took out a few booklets and worksheets from her backpack. Then she grabbed a legal pad and listed academic things she could do while school was out. I know that taking control of the situation made her feel much better. I also felt hopeful that she would follow through so she wouldn't feel this badly again. Truth be told, some of that list was accomplished and some of it wasn't. My daughter is still quite young, so working with her on accountability and intrinsic motivation is going to be a work in progress.

How does my daughter's story relate to you? Take inventory of your emotions around failing. Label them. You deserve to feel good about yourself and about being in school. You deserve to have the support mechanisms available to you. Formulate your plan, and then follow through with that plan so you can avoid the painful feelings associated with failure. The good news is that those exact feelings can also inspire you to make lasting changes.

I know that you can.

The Career Note

I asked Shawn Murphy, the best-selling author of *The Optimistic Workplace*, "How can building a support system while in college benefit a student once they're in the workplace?" He replied:

> *Pride, shame, or vulnerability trick our minds to hide the very things that trigger these emotions. We become isolated from those we love, trust, even admire. The workplace is not impervious to experiences that will trigger similar responses.*
>
> *Meaningful, trusting relationships are central to help make sense of situations where pride, shame, or vulnerability rears its nasty head. We need relationships that help us realize our potential. These are the people who can help us flourish. Who will hold us accountable and help us through whatever struggles we face. And they do so without judgment or blame. Meaningful, trusting relationships are the counterbalance to the muck and grind that threatens to minimize us and our work. How fortunate is the person who can experience life surrounded by a rich network of friends, colleagues, mentors, teachers, and advisors?*
>
> Shawn, business consultant & author

Classroom/Peers

3. ■ Disrupting the Class

What You Might Think:

I was so funny in high school.

What Your Professor Thinks:

Your funny should never disrupt my class.

The Real Story

Jake and Marshall made an impression within the first few minutes of class.

Just as I introduced myself—as in, I had just said my name—Jake raised his hand and asked, "Are you gay?"

I am rarely speechless, but in that moment, I had nothing. The fun didn't stop there.

After reviewing the syllabus, students formed small groups for our first-day activity. Jake and Marshall stuck together, and I was too much of a novice to realize that I should have counted students off to separate these guys.

Suddenly, I heard a wave of laughter. There was Marshall, lying face-down on one of the long tables. A few students shook their heads in disgust.

I walked over, bent down to face Marshall, and cocked my head. "Five a.m. drills on the soccer team, right?"

"Yeah," he said. "This morning."

"I'd be toast," I replied. "Can you sit in your seat for a bit?"

I set the precedence of a doormat, but getting the kid upright was my main goal at that moment.

The antics ended that day. The duo rushed out the door, and I found myself surrounded by five other students.

"They're just like they were in high school," a student remarked.

Another student said, "I can't give a speech in front of those guys." Two other students nodded.

Great. Public speaking is stressful. How could I blame these students for their concern? If Jake and Marshall could taunt me on the first day, anyone could be a target.

I assured the students I would handle the situation. The next day, Jake and Marshall came in a few minutes late. Jake went up and sat at my computer.

I gave him a sharp look and pointed to his seat. Was I was dealing with a college student?

"I need to speak with you after class," I went over and whispered.

I heard other students: "Those guys are idiots." "They pull this crap in Dr. W's class all the time." "They've been hit in the head with too many soccer balls."

Jake and Marshall were infecting my class. I couldn't let it continue. Later, I sat down with Jake and Marshall and said,

"Guys, I love your energy, but the comments ... the computer ... This behavior is disruptive. Some students feel intimidated to give a speech in front of you. Like you might make fun of them."

Marshall looked incredulous. "Like we'd really mess up someone else's speech."

"Well, the other students in the class don't know that," I replied. "But this has to stop."

Jake and Marshall assured me they wouldn't create a problem. And they didn't. Sort of.

They still responded to open questions inappropriately.

They still engaged in side talk far more often than they should have.

They were barely focused during speeches.

So, they were still creating a "mood" for my class. And that mood wasn't good.

Distraction comes in other forms besides class clowning. Two different students, Giancarlo and Niema, were engaged in an ongoing conversation throughout my class. Despite my calm and, finally, direct request to be quiet, they wouldn't stop. Niema started crying. She was embarrassed I called them out. That took time and energy away from almost a full class session.

If students don't want to be called out (and believe me, I try everything before that's necessary), then, really, they need to be more thoughtful about their conduct to begin with!

The Backstory

Put yourself in your professor's shoes. If you stood in front of a classroom every day, trying to be interesting, engaging, and informative (but mostly engaging, or else students will zone out or fall asleep), you'd know that it takes a tremendous amount of effort to make Every. Single. Class. Session. that way.

From a student's perspective, I get the high-school admiration if you're like Jake and Marshall. Why wouldn't you want to be that same hero in college? After all, you probably got many people through an otherwise boring class. You may have felt admired because you were seen as bold and confident.

In college, that over-the-top behavior is viewed as immature by other students. The situation becomes a huge energy drain for professors and can hurt the entire class tone, despite the professor's goal of a comfortable and enjoyable class environment. I had to be on guard with Jake and Marshall, which I am sure was evident in some of my palpable tension.

Shifting to Giancarlo and Niema, perpetual side talk is just plain annoying. This also distracts other students sitting close by, which is why the professor has to take quick action to shut it down. Also, once two students engage in conversation, then others take that as their lead to start. It's sort of like when a student pulls out a phone (I'll discuss tech distraction in Chapter 22). Other students take the cue that they can do the same.

A professor doesn't have to put up with classroom disruption of any type. Some professors might shame the offenders (I'm not saying this is right), or kick them out of class and file a report based on the official college Student Code of Conduct. Every college has a policy to deal with disruptive behavior, and the consequences can be severe.

Ask Yourself This:

Was I funny all the time in high school? What did I gain from this behavior (e.g., I felt good about myself. I believed that others liked me. I felt accepted. I felt funny.)? Do I expect to get the same benefits in college? Why do I engage in side talk? What am I missing when I am distracting and don't pay attention in class?

Think This:

I need to create a good reputation with professors and peers in college. It's time to get serious. I can show that I'm fun without being over the top.

Not That:

I'm getting a lot of attention, which will keep me popular like I was in high school.

If other people are willing to chat with me during class, this means I'm popular, so I'd better go for it.

You don't want to be popular for all the wrong reasons. You won't see other students talking about your craziness, but they will. They'll complain to others or to the professor.

Say This (to yourself):

I'm ready to give up the act and find my new self in college. People will like me for who I am now.

And say this to your professor, if you've created some "interesting" behavior already:

I have done some distracting things and I realize I need to change my behavior immediately.

You don't need to say much else. Your professor will get it. If he has something else to say about your behavior, he will. Listen, try not to get defensive, and just reiterate that you're ready to be serious.

I've already acted up, so I can't really change any-one's opinion anyway.

Not true. Make tomorrow a new day. Go to class; be friendly without being over the top. Use your wit to engage appropri-ately in class discussion. Your peers and professors will appreci-ate the shift, even if they don't respond positively right away. They may want to see if this "new you" is going to stick.

The End Note

The situation with Jake and Marshall never resolved. I went to their soccer coach for advice, but they were already in too much trouble from similar behavior in other classes.

Before class the next day, Jake said, "You ratted us out!"

I asked the coach to give me advice, *not* to destroy my relationship with these students (even though they had almost done that on their own).

"I didn't rat you out," I said. "Your coach does a monthly progress check. I was left with no other choice but to ask his advice on what to do."

Jake spoke, but Marshall stood by, arms folded. "We've been told not to open our mouths again in your class."

And that was it. Jake and Marshall participated only when necessary. They stared at the wall the rest of the time. Their silence made teaching easier for me, but the class never achieved a "relaxed" environment.

What was sad is that behind the fun and games were two excellent speakers. Had their behavior not spoken so loudly, they had such value to add to our class.

Jake and Marshall entered college but had no clue about how to make a positive impression. If you are some version of these students, ditch that persona. Decide that you are ready to find the grown-up version of yourself.

What will that look like? Come to class on time, ready to learn. If you're late, set your things down quietly and take a seat in back so as not to disrupt the professor. Be friendly or at least cordial to others around you. Put away your phone and look like you are ready to learn. You don't have to sit in front of the class—you can be engaged from anywhere in the class—but do engage. Raise your hand and attempt to answer questions. When your professor puts you in groups or pairs, talk with others and stay on track with the activity or discussion. And be careful about distractions. Avoid whispering or using tech during class (again, this will be a separate chapter).

Remember: classroom impressions count. You never know who will be in future classes with you, and of course, you want your professor to see you as a professional. So present yourself just that way.

The Career Note:

Hopefully, class jokers or disrupters have gotten this out of their systems by the time they reach the workplace. But what if that doesn't happen? I had these questions: Have you experienced a coworker who distracted or disrupted the team? What would the reprimand or consequence be if this behavior continued?

> *A few years ago, I was working on a project with a cross-functional group. One guy was always trying to be funny, making off-topic comments and jokes. He was new to the company, and initially everyone gave him some room to settle in, not knowing if the behavior was an expression of him feeling ill at ease*

or truly a personality facet. We realized soon enough that it wasn't going to stop without some intervention, but usually a simple redirection would shut it down: "Thanks for that aside, Matt, but let's get back to the matter at hand" or a light "Appreciate the feedback, but if we need to, let's discuss that offline." I think if redirection hadn't worked, a private discussion about staying on task would have been next. He was a great guy and definitely able to contribute to the team, but his tic of making jokes and going off topic was a reflex he had to unlearn. In the long run, I think that behavior can affect your career prospects, because folks won't want to work with you or take you seriously.

Kristin, biopharmaceuticals

4. Calling the Professor Out/ Challenging the Professor

What You Might Think:

I am paying for this education. If I don't agree with my professor's lecture, opinion, whatever, I have the right to call her out.

What Your Professor Thinks:

Where is the respect? Challenging me is one thing, but calling me out in front of everyone? Not appropriate.

The Real Story

When you stand up in front of students as often as most professors do, there are times when we may come across as confusing. (You're probably thinking that's more often than not).

For example, if I am trying out a new lesson, assignment, etc., there are times when I may unintentionally confuse my students. Last year, I assigned a new worksheet for students to build their speech outlines. It appeared similar to another worksheet they were already completing. In my mind, one would build on another, giving me more opportunity to help with a high-stakes and difficult assignment.

When I explained the two worksheets, my students looked perplexed, so I laughed (nervously) and said, "I am sorry. I guess I can be confusing sometimes."

One student, Janet, said loudly and snidely, "Yes, you definitely can!"

I could feel my face getting hot. I am rarely speechless, but in that moment, while I didn't lose my composure, I definitely lost my words.

On a different occasion, Mick came into class asking if we would stay for the entire session. I said, "Well, today is our last day of speeches, so I suppose that will depend on how long they take."

"I really need to leave early today," Mick replied anxiously. "There's something I need to take care of."

Mick had already missed quite a bit of class due to various mild medical issues. Since I finally had him in class, I wanted him to stay there.

I had Mick do the usual audience "job" of evaluating two other students' speeches. Once he was finished, he asked me out loud if he could leave. I told him he could do what he needed to do, but that it would be unfair to everyone else if I gave permission for him to go.

Mick became visibly frustrated. "I have done what I was supposed to do, and I really need to leave now! Why do you need me to stay?"

This time, I didn't feel embarrassed. I was mad. These conversations don't belong in front of twenty-five-plus other students, and I had already accommodated Mick in every possible way.

"I'm sorry, Mick," I said as calmly as I could. "I have to ask that we discuss this at a different time. Not in front of the class, and definitely not during speeches."

The Backstory

When I chose this line of work, I promised myself that I'd never be that professor who embarrasses students. I had professors like that: when I was in college, one of my psychology professors locked the door after class started. If you were late, you wore something around your neck for the duration of the class. I've blocked out what the "something" was.

Being a professor who strives to be respectful doesn't mean that I won't get my share of "vinegar" from time to time. When it happens, I feel surprised, hurt, and angry; angry at myself for feeling vulnerable, and angry at the outspoken student for being so openly disrespectful.

I am human. When unfriendly fire comes my way in front of a class, certainly my inclination is to save myself from embarrassment. So what I wanted to say to each of these students was "Cut me some slack! I'm giving you two opportunities for feedback. Do you know how much work that is for me? Or that not every professor does this?" and "Are you kidding me? You've missed one-third of this class, and I've worked with you the whole time. Now you're giving me grief because I won't give you permission to leave?"

But I didn't say any of that. Instead, I did what professors are supposed to do: I reinflated myself and continued the day's events.

Now, of course, this is just my perspective. You might say I'm overly sensitive, and you wouldn't be wrong. Some professors may ignore these kinds of comments altogether, letting them roll right off their back. Others will respond and possibly not in a very kind way.

The point is that whether the professor is being confusing or you don't like what he has to say, speaking in a sarcastic or rude manner doesn't get anyone's needs met. Sure, you may momentarily embarrass the professor or rile them up (which might be your goal), but your problem won't get solved quickly. Alternatively, others in the class may see you as someone who is disrespectful or aggressive—even if they agree with what you are saying.

Ask Yourself This:

What am I trying to achieve by calling out my professor? Have I been successful in the past when I've tried this approach? Have I considered the long-term ramifications of speaking out to a professor in front of the whole class?

Think This:

I have the right to challenge my professor if I disagree with a fact or opinion. I can get my point across in a professional way. If I am confused about something, I deserve to have clarification. I am more likely to get the answers if I approach the situation in a nonconfrontational way.

Not That:

I am an adult and I'll say what I want. It's the professor's problem if they don't like it.

True. The professor can choose how he responds to what you are saying. However, realize that you may be burning a bridge. And, in the time it takes for your professor to overcome frustration with your approach, he could have been solving your problem.

Say This:

I have a different take on the situation. I'd like to share that, if you don't mind.

I thought I learned that fact a little differently. Tell me if you've heard this.

The instructions are still not clear to me. Could you be more specific about the third section?

Super important: your words can sound nonconfrontational, but if your tone is still sarcastic, you won't come across as calmly and professionally as you'd like.

Not That:

You're wrong about that!

You're confusing me/everyone.

You have the right to feel like your professor is wrong. You have the right to feel frustrated because you are confused. Just focus on getting your message across while not being perceived as someone who lets their emotions get in the way.

The End Note

The day that I was called out by Janet, I had already planned to have some quick one-on-one meetings with each student to discuss upcoming speeches. When I reached Janet, I could feel my pulse quicken. I wondered if she'd continue telling me how confusing I was. The second I pulled over my chair, she huffed, "I'm really stressed because our speeches are due in a week."

"Your speeches are due in *two* weeks," I said.

"Wait ... what?"

She smiled, put her hand on her heart, and rocked back in her chair.

I couldn't help myself: "So, um, that whole thing before was about this?"

"Yeah," she said, looking remorseful.

I nodded and said, "Good to know. Because I have to tell you, that felt pretty harsh."

"I'm so sorry," she said, genuinely. "I didn't mean it that way. I love this class."

"I understand. I appreciate knowing where it was coming from."

And I did.

In Mick's situation, I didn't get the opportunity to address him other than in e-mail. After all, I couldn't be sure that he'd come back to class the next day.

I wrote, "I understand that you obviously needed to leave early the other day. I need you to look at this from my perspective: you've missed one-third of the class, and I've worked with you the whole time. You were finally back in class, and I didn't want you to miss any more. Out of fairness, I also couldn't just give you permission to leave without potentially upsetting others. Getting so frustrated about this in front of the whole class set an uncomfortable tone on an already stressful day of giving speeches."

To my surprise, Mick replied, "Nothing further needs to be said. I acted inappropriately and I will apologize to the class."

I never asked for Mick to do this, but, indeed, he sent an e-mail to everyone saying that he was sorry for being so impatient.

I have to tell you that, just as much as students sometimes feel wronged and misunderstood, instructors can feel like punching bags, too. Some professors feel like students are just waiting to verbally pounce. On both sides, there is nothing to be gained by harshness, even when it may feel "good" and tension-relieving to speak that way. Remember that in both situations above, the students ultimately realized that they were out of line and voluntarily made amends.

I don't want to end this section without mentioning that you might find yourself on the other end of this dynamic: some professors speak in an abrupt, sarcastic, or generally off-putting way. My advice is still the same: keep your end goal in mind. Keep your emotions and your professionalism in check. Always make sure that whatever communication is coming your way, you remained collected and composed. In any situation, that will give you the upper hand, even if it doesn't feel that way at the time.

The Career Note

I wondered, "How are employees who are openly critical of superiors, the company at large, or colleagues perceived in the workplace? What challenges would these employees face?" I asked a retail merchandising expert:

Try not to openly (or internally) criticize anyone at work. You cannot predict how someone will react to negative feedback or being challenged. If you keep criticism constructive with the goal of helping that person, you can predict and even control the outcome, to some degree. This creates opportunity and loyalty, and gives you instant value.

Employees who are disrespectful are not seen as team players who can work in global business. Companies need people who love what they do, who they are doing it with, and who they are doing it for.

In my early career, I was at times outspoken and hard to work with. I lost creative people on my staff, and I found myself doing a hundred jobs because I created an impossible environment for people to take initiative or feel confident in their jobs. It took me a long time to realize that I was better, more creative, and more successful when I was a positive force to be reckoned with rather than just a force to be dealt with. Once I learned to challenge myself in a positive way, I made huge, progressive leaps and lifelong connections that serve me in my career to this day.

Nicolette, retail executive

5. Being a Spokesperson for Others in Class

What You Might Say:

"Everybody is confused about that writing assignment."

What Your Professor Thinks:

Telling me how other students feel doesn't help you.

The Real Story

Outspoken, outgoing Valeria came to see me during office hours over an assignment that she felt unsure about. Valeria entered my office with a gritty look on her face. She plopped in the chair next to my desk.

"I don't get the requirements for this persuasive speech," Valeria said.

I wait for a second or two like an expectant puppy, hoping she'll give me more information, but she doesn't. Finally, I asked, "Can you be more specific?"

"I don't get where we're supposed to refute opposition. I'm confused about the format." She pauses for a minute. "And you know what? A bunch of other people are frustrated and confused, too. We needed more time to go over the structure of this speech in class."

I replied: "I really appreciate you telling me about *your* confusion, Valeria, and I'm sorry that you're feeling frustrated. Let's break down the format so we can get you moving ahead on this speech and feeling good about it."

The Backstory

Students come to me with all sorts of personal issues. Megan had a death in the family. She now raises her young siblings and barely has time to do any schoolwork, yet she desperately wants to finish college. Hiro feels uncomfortable raising his hand in class because this is not typical in his Taiwanese culture. He'd rather e-mail me his thoughts privately. Alec has just finished a tour of duty in Iraq and can't stop drinking.

While students often share their own problems openly, students almost never discuss another student's personal life. The same does *not* ring true when the student has a class-related problem. Then, the student who is frustrated, confused, etc., becomes the spokesperson for every other student who shares the same frustration or confusion.

Of course, students don't tell me who is having the problem, so when I hear, "A bunch of other people don't understand this assignment either," I'm not exactly sure how many "a bunch" is.

It could be two students or fifteen, or maybe the whole class is lost. Maybe I've perplexed the entire college!

I certainly understand the spokesperson's need to make it sound like they are crowd-supported. After all, complaining to a professor feels scary and embarrassing when the student believes that she *should* understand the information. Likewise, some students feel angry over an assignment or a grade, and they want the professor to know that many other students share their opinion.

I absolutely want students to come to me for help. I'd much prefer students e-mail me or visit me every single day than silently suffer and stress out. Sure, I know that students talk to each other and voice their frustrations about grades, work, and, yes, even about me. However, when a student is sitting in front of me, I can only help *that* student with his own problem.

Think about it: even if the student polled everyone in the class, and every single one of their classmates agreed they didn't like something, I can't help everyone through one student. What's that "spokes student" going to do—return to the class with a megaphone and say, "I handled the problem. We're all good now!"?

Let's say a bunch of Valeria's classmates don't understand that same persuasive speech format. It's a tough project, so the fact that more than one student is struggling doesn't surprise me. However, if Valeria tells me people are confused about the format, that's too vague. Some students might be confused about opposition/refutation. Others might not know what to do with the visualization step. A few may not know how to handle transitions. Everyone's "confusion over the format" may look very different. This is why I need to hear from individual students about their own frustration/confusion/concern.

Another thought: if a flurry of students suddenly swarms into my office needing assistance, those masses will tell me that I need to a) give more instruction for the assignment; or b) give more time for the assignment. Professors are hardwired to realize that if one student needs help, there are probably three others who need it, too.

Ask Yourself This:

> *Why am I telling my professor that everyone else is confused? Do I feel embarrassed about the fact that I'm not getting it? Do I feel like the professor won't take me seriously?*

Also ask:

> *Have I previously told teachers about how others think/feel so I can have more basis for my own argument? Did saying this make any difference in getting help for myself?*

Think This:

> *If my classmates are confused, I'm not totally clueless or going crazy. But even though we are all in the same boat, the professor can get each of us unstuck and moving forward. I can and should only vouch for myself and encourage others to do the same.*

It's validating to know that you aren't alone in your frustration or confusion. However, talking to your colleagues doesn't break you out of the confusion bubble. That's your professor's job.

Not That:

> If I tell my professor that everyone is confused, I won't look like the only one. The professor will think it's a big problem.

The second a student tells me how "everybody feels," they actually water down their own need for help, and their peers miss an opportunity to get personalized assistance.

Say This:

> Professor, I'm confused about our upcoming persuasive speech format.

Then be specific about what you're struggling with:

> I'm having trouble figuring out if my thesis statement will work. I'm also not sure where the transitions go, and I don't know how to insert my opposition in the right place.

After you get the help you need, you can also say to your professor, "That makes far more sense to me now. Maybe you can share this with the whole class in case others are confused." (The professor will likely agree with you!).

Then, say to your colleagues, "If you're not sure about what's going on, go talk to the professor during office hours. I did and was able to get just what I needed to move ahead on this assignment."

Not That:

> Everybody else isn't getting this!
>
> *or*
>
> I know a bunch of other students don't think the grades were fair either!

The second you bring up how everyone else feels/thinks, you've just taken time—and credibility—away from getting help for yourself. This is one time where being self-centered and focusing on what *you* need is absolutely okay.

The End Note

In college, you don't need to represent the opinions of others. You only need to represent yourself. Your thoughts and concerns matter, regardless of whether everyone else or no one else shares them. There is power in numbers, but in this case, far more power in individual numbers. Explain your concerns. Encourage your classmates to do the same. Then, you can come together again to help each other.

The Career Note

I wondered how a spokesperson is perceived in the workplace and what happens when an employee rallies for others or bolsters their own complaints by using other people's concerns—instead of focusing on his/her own issue:

> *This happens quite a bit in the workplace. In my career in the insurance industry, it happened often. I am one of those people who are passionate, I love to talk and dispute things, and I love being an*

advocate for others. Because of this, my personality draws people to me for advice, support, and the "go-to" to talk to the instructor, manager, or supervisor. I'm not afraid to speak my mind and I often wonder why others don't feel the same way. I know when I have rallied around others, the first thing I see and hear from my boss is a concern as to why the others can't come forward and talk as I am willing to do. All I can say is everyone is different and has their own ghosts to deal with. What I have found is if there is a strong boss, he or she hears what I have to say and, together, we come up with a plan to make changes. If the boss has low self esteem, they may take offense that I came forward and that my peers are fearful of talking to them. I have seen this happen both ways.

Marianne, youth development, nonprofit

6. Dealing with Group Work

What You Might Think:

Group work sucks. Either I end up doing all the work, someone slacks off, or my grade goes down because others just don't care.

What Your Professor Thinks:

Group work may suck, but I assign it because it's important real-world practice for you.

The Real Story

You've probably lived the "real story" already in one work group or another that didn't meet your expectations, or one that downright sucked. Perhaps your grade suffered, or it didn't only because you did all the work. Perhaps others standards weren't up to your own, and you felt alone. Perhaps you wondered why you have to deal with group work at all.

The Backstory

Why in the heck do professors assign group work, anyway? The most obvious answer? To provide you with real-world experience. As of this book's writing, here are passages from three real job descriptions in medical, general business, and tech industries:

> This position will work closely with the application teams in ensuring that requirements are correctly defined and administered.

> Enthusiastic team player, productive working independently or as part of a group; ability to interface effectively with all levels of the organization.

> Ideal candidate will have the ability to collaborate across functions and business groups to drive consensus.

Hundreds of other job descriptions contain variations of these phrases. Therefore, that exceptional or lousy group experience can give you critical career practice and a tangible example when you're asked the inevitable "So, tell me about a time you successfully worked on a team."

You're probably wondering how a poor group experience can do anything for you, other than give you heartache. Let me paint a picture: one of my colleagues uses a ton of group projects in class, and one group imploded by their second meeting. Two members openly berated a peer for not getting the reading done. They didn't even let the student speak, but instead just berated him. The student got up and walked away.

My colleague stepped in, first approaching the alienated member and then leading the whole group in a problem-solving conversation to get them back on track.

Those students all gained experience that day. Each could reflect upon this situation in an interview, saying, "I could have handled that situation differently in college. Here's what I would do now."

Great potential work experience doesn't help your miserable feelings while the group situation is going on. I get that. You may feel fully responsible to fix the issues and at the same time help-less to solve them. You may worry heavily about your grade.

Professors feel your pain, too. We know that group work is highly stressful, and we worry right along with you about problems. With all its bumps, you aren't likely to escape group work in college. Instead, focus on managing your experience and communicate in the most professional way. Here are recommendations:

Don't run to your professor immediately. I will tell you when it is time to do that, but attempt to problem solve first. Many professors, like the colleague I mentioned above, keep close tabs on students' groups, swiftly intervening at the sign of a problem. Others let students sink, swim, and figure things out. Try the latter.

Take leader-type actions from the start. Put the onus on yourself to get the ball rolling. You don't have to be a dictator to assertively take charge, and helping the conversation start doesn't mean you'll be the default leader. You could say, "I'll take notes on everyone's ideas for our topic. Here's one idea to start us off …" or "I'll lead the discussion this time, and Joe, why don't you take it next time?"

If someone is the discussion leader and note taker at every meeting, then there is clear and documented accountability for group members "owning" what they agree to do.

Establish clear deadlines and backup plans. Ask each person to set their deadline *with* group agreement. The date should allow a couple days' breathing room if something needs to be modified. Ask each person about their backup plan if something goes wrong (on the early deadline—not the day before the assignment is due).

Say, "Given that we only have a week (two weeks, whatever) to pull all this together, if one of us misses a deadline, can we agree that they will get one reminder, then someone else will have to take over that job?" Make sure that new person is ready to move quickly.

Agree on the end goal. Everyone needs to be in *specific* agreement about expected quality of work. Is it an A? If so, what does A work look like? Underperforming can be as bad as not performing. Assign yourself or ask someone else to be "quality control" to make sure the outcome is up to standards.

A separate agreement should establish how the group is evaluated or how the grade is divided should everyone not do their fair share (or if someone's work can't be submitted due to low quality). This is dependent, of course, on how your professor set up the project to begin with. Even if your professor doesn't ask for group members to evaluate each other, if the work is unbalanced or if you have nonperformers, you can propose to the functioning group members: "If someone needs to take over someone else's work, I suggest we submit a group evaluation along with this project."

Right the "wrongs" proactively. If things seem to be going sideways, get everyone back together before they fall apart. Reestablish everyone's deliverables and the due dates. You can say: "We agreed that Nyara would have X done by Monday evening and Mike would have X done by Wednesday, and I will update where we are on Thursday."

You're probably wondering what to do if Nyara and Mike become slackers. What do you do then? I don't recommend a dramatic intervention. No one has time for that. You can attempt one private conversation to be diplomatic: "The group is concerned about you. Is there something going on that is preventing you from getting this work done? What is your plan to complete your part?"

Realize that unless the nonproducer starts producing, what they say doesn't negate the fact that the work needs to be done. If the person has a genuine life issue, they need to speak with the professor. If they are just slacking, you won't have time for empty promises and more delay.

I can't emphasize enough to keep the drama out of your group situation as much as you can. You don't have time to go back and forth with accusations and behind-the-back talk. That will just drain your energy and reduce group morale.

Make sure *all* group decisions about next steps are transparent. Keep the slacking group member in the loop: include them in e-mail exchanges, even if they don't respond. You'll have documentation that you tried to include them.

All that said, you should never be forced to carry someone else's weight at the expense of your grade. In business, there would be harsh ramifications if someone did not do their share of the work, and your boss would likely get involved.

Keep everything "business" as much as you can. The slacker will learn soon enough that working this way just doesn't work. Hopefully your professor will make things equitable in the end.

Ask Yourself This:

How do I feel about working in groups? What made things go well in groups I've been part of? What made things go wrong in groups that were dysfunctional? How have I handled problems in groups in the past?

Think This:

I can't control other members in the group. I can only control myself. There are steps I can take if group members aren't doing their fair share.

Not That:

I need to do all of this myself because that's the only way it's going to get done. I shouldn't be working in groups anyway.

I know that many people feel like they'd prefer to work alone. Dealing with yourself is far more predictable. No one said you have to love working in groups, although there can actually be great benefits in collaborating with others. Knowing how to manage group dynamics is where you can show your talent, and that quality is something employers definitely look for!

Say This:

What kind of evaluation will the group submit once the project is finished? Will we be able to grade or rate other members' performance?

If you are not told to turn in some sort of evaluation, say, "I just wanted to let you know that in my group, we had some issues. We established clear tasks and deadlines, but we needed to reorganize our group members' responsibilities in a few places to get the work done. We were able to solve the problems but would like to submit a formal group evaluation."

Your professor will hopefully agree that it is not fair for everyone to receive the same grade if only three of four people carried the work—unless everyone agrees to that, of course.

Not That:

I hate group work and don't understand why you are making us do this.

or

Fail the slacker's ass so the rest of us get As!

As long as you are professional in your recount of what happened in your group, the professor will already see that you're looking for fairness. If she has specific questions, she'll ask or gather together with your group.

The End Note

I realize that sometimes it may seem easier to just work on your own rather than deal with a group—particularly when people can be unpredictable. If you think about it, group work will remain a huge part of your life, not just in your career, but also in so many other types of situations. Maybe you'll do volunteer work that involves team dynamics, or you'll work with neighbors to organize a block party, or you'll drive your future kids in a carpool. All of these situations involve group dynamics.

This is yet another time that I am going to tell you to be selfish! Think of the communication practice that group work can afford you. You can't ever control other people, their behaviors, intentions, or goals, but you can control yours. If you know how to professionally and assertively work in a team capacity, then that security will help you feel confident about working in any situation with others. That is the exact marketable skill you need to sell to an employer or in a promotion!

The Career Note

When I considered an industry expert on team dynamics in the workplace, I sought out a regular LinkedIn and *Inc.com* columnist and author of the *New York Times* best seller *Likeable Social Media* and the newly released *The Art of People*. I asked about the correlation between the way a student might behave in a class work group versus a workplace group. Here's what I learned:

> *There is definitely a correlation between classrelated behavior in groups and how those students function in a group in the workplace. Students who do most of the work will likely become employees who do most of the work in their organizations. Still, group experiences in college provide a terrific and rare opportunity to truly prepare students for what's to come in the business world. They can and should use these experiences to work on their people skills—listening, understanding, collaborating, and persuading their way to greater success.*

> *Dave, social media/business*

Grades

7. Comparing Grades with Others

What You Might Say:

Joe got a 92, and I only got an 88. I have more positive comments than he does!

What Your Professor Thinks:

I can't talk about Joe's grade. But I can explain why you received your grade.

The Real Story

Polina came to see me during office hours with a graded assignment in hand.

"I don't understand," she said. "Why did I get an 88 and someone else got a 92? The other person has similar checkmarks on the score sheet!"

"Let me take a look," I said. "But I can't discuss anyone else's grade with you, only yours."

Another student, Clint, caught me after class a few days later. "I'm okay with my grade," he said. "But I heard a bunch of other speeches that I thought were worse than mine."

"So you want to discuss why you earned your grade?" I asked.

"No. I know why I got it."

I clearly remembered Clint's feedback sheet. He received a high C because his content was lacking references, even though his delivery was quite strong. On top of that, he lost 5 points for going significantly over time.

Several students in Clint's class received a C for various reasons, so I never fully understood Clint's basis for comparison.

The Backstory

I totally get it. When I was a student, I compared, too. How can you resist? You get that paper or test back from your professor and are salivating with curiosity: what did other people get? Did they do better than you? What about that guy who said he wrote the paper that morning? How'd he do?

I personally think that we are more hardwired for comparison than ever! Think about the images bombarding us from social media: other people are taking better trips, eating better food—living better lives!

A dear communication colleague of mine, Rob Walsh, has a great saying: "Comparison is the fast track to misery." He's totally right. Every time I've compared myself to someone else, if the outcome wasn't ideal, I'd feel so much worse about myself.

While your response to social media comparisons might be based in emotions, your desire to rationalize a grade is completely reasonable. Just don't look for that rationale in another student. Turn to your professor. Your professor should be able to offer you rubrics, checklists, a detailed assignment description, etc., so your grade outcome is concrete rather than seemingly random.

However, when you teach in a more subjective area like I do, all the rubrics in the world may still not clarify why two students can have the same grade or a slightly different grade, but still have similar checkmarks or circled rubric items.

Let me give you an example. A student receives a C on a speech for these reasons:

- Decent delivery but minimal sources, no sources, or clearly uncredible sources.

- Reading 70 percent of the speech, even with strong content.

- Going short on time, leaving out a source, and having decent delivery.

- Going long on time, tedious delivery (reading, stalls), decent content.

So you can see, two students can earn a C, but for entirely different reasons. And one student may receive a B or low B if one of these variables changes (i.e., meeting the time, leaving out one source, and having decent delivery).

Students can only fully understand their grade if I write specific comments. Circling numbers on a checklist or rubric doesn't tell the whole story. Therefore, when a student comes to me pissed off about their grade, I refer them to what I wrote on the feedback form.

I always tell students that their grade is not determined on the best work in the class. Instead, their grade is based on:

- The assignment requirements and standards;

- Their own level of mastery (in other words, how well or not well they did), based on the assignment requirements and standards;

- And sometimes, their individual improvement on a series of similar assignments.

I realize that I may not be able to convince you not to compare your grades with others, but please, before you do, get the facts! Ask for anything that you can get your hands on to tell you how the professor grades. Ask for a checklist, rubric, score sheet, samples of previous student work, etc. You must have this well before your submission deadline. Once you know what is expected of you, hopefully your grade will become clear.

Remember, if you are unsure about the grade you received, or if you happened to find out someone else's grade and are now upset about your own, then the only person who can help is your professor. Your classmates can commiserate with you, but they can't give you the answers about your grade.

Silently seething is no better and will ultimately work against you. You'll have a hard time focusing, and you'll dread going to class. Your future grades could suffer. If you are upset about your grade, whether based on someone else's outcome or a grade you didn't expect, don't swallow your anger and expect it to get better. Get the insight from your professor.

Ask Yourself This:

What do I hope to gain by asking others about their grades? How will I handle it if I find out I didn't do as well? How have I felt in the past when I've compared my grades? Did I take action based on what I learned?

Think This:

My grade is the only one that matters. If I'm not happy with my grade, finding out others' grades isn't going to change my frustration. I can take control of this situation. I can talk to my professor and discuss my concerns. If I choose to ask others about their grades, or if I happen to find out, I can't let this information impact my possibilities for success.

Not That:

The professor likes Monica better than me, so she got a better grade.

Believe it or not, professors do not grade on personality.

or

I'm not as smart as Reynaldo, and that's why I didn't do as well.

Just because someone received a better grade doesn't reflect your intelligence. An undesirable grade is a snapshot of work based on a set of prescribed requirements. An undesirable grade isn't a snapshot of your overall abilities as a person or your potential to succeed on the next assignment. I know it feels that way, but turn that negativity into fire: the fire to get the help you need for next time!

Say This:

Before the assignment, if you haven't received these assignments, ask:

> Do you have any rubrics, samples, checklists, examples, or further explanations of how you'll be grading our work?

You can add:

> Will you review work in advance? How early do you need to receive my draft?

If you've received your grade already, say:

> I'd like more specific feedback on what lowered my score for this assignment.

If you cannot resist the urge to admit that you saw someone else's grade, say:

> I know it isn't a good idea to compare my grade with others. I know Selwyn got a 92. I thought I did at least as well as he did. Can you explain why my grade was lower?

Remember, you will get answers about your grade, but due to confidentiality, your instructor cannot discuss the other student's score.

Not That:

> I don't understand why three other people got a higher grade! What did they do that I didn't?

Lead with your concerns about *your* grade. Being confrontational and asking about someone else's grade sends the message that you believe the professor is unfair and grading on personal likes and dislikes. You want to maintain a positive relationship, even if you disagree about your grade. Handle the situation professionally.

End Note

If I've convinced you not to compare grades with others, this does not mean that someone won't turn the tables and try to compare with you! If that happens, don't get sucked into their grade world. Instead, advise that the professor can tell them what they need to know.

The Career Note

I wondered how comparison plays out in the workplace, so I asked a retail store owner who previously worked in global medical devices:

> *Many employees don't compare performance reviews or salary to protect privacy. Some don't worry about this and then a few things can happen: the lesser performing employee may work harder for a better review next time—the best case scenario. More realistically, a manager will know that privacy was breached, and they now have to use precious*

work time/resources trying to substantiate the review or salary difference. Also, the manager knows the employee is unhappy and may become difficult (e.g., perform fewer tasks, demonstrate laziness, be unwilling to accept new tasks, etc.) or even leave. From there, a manager must be prepared to document the employee's declining performance so they are legally covered in case the employee threatens discrimination or another injustice. It's human nature to wonder about other people's salary and performance, but, really, an employee should just focus on their own performance and keep communication open with the manager regarding potential improvement opportunities. Leave others out of it.

Mark, retail store owner

8.

Your Grades, Part 1:
"Giving" Them, "Needing" Them, and Working "Hard" for Them

*Note: Grades are a huge topic! I'm going to break up this chapter up into two parts. Part 1 will take you through **The Real Story** and **The Backstory**. Part 2 will give you tips on what to say to deal with grade matters.*

What You Might Say:

Why did you give me a 3.0? I needed a 3.5 in this class so it will transfer to my university! I worked really hard for it!

or

I'm sitting at a 3.3 right now. Can you just give me the other .2 to get my GPA up?

What Your Professor Thinks:

I don't give grades, you earned them. Hard work doesn't guarantee a grade. If you "needed" a 3.5, we should have had that conversation in week one, not week fourteen.

The Real Story:

"Tell me about your grade goals immediately," I tell my students on the *first day*. "Don't wait until the end of the term, when it's already too late."

Seizing this opportunity, Dmitri and Ana came to see me on the class break. Ana spoke first: "Um, you said that if we need a certain grade, we should tell you early. I need a 4.0." Dmitri nodded in agreement.

I told Dmitri and Ana to focus on written work first. Strong grades on written outlines can improve actual speech grades. If they showed me their work seventy-two hours before the deadline, I would give feedback (not every professor is willing). The students said they'd take my advice. I hoped that they would.

Now fast forward: same class, end of term. Two different students.

Dane earned a D, and Sarah, a B.

Dane missed a bunch of small assignments, and those points added up. He did not do well on his speech outlines, although his speech delivery was high-B range. Dane never checked on his grades throughout the term.

Sarah's work was far more solid than Dane's. She submitted everything, but she read a lot of her speeches rather than using a conversational tone. She was just shy of A-level work.

When Dane saw his grade, he e-mailed and said, "So, is this the final grade? Is there anything I can do? I needed to do better than this."

I responded, "We needed to have this conversation eight weeks ago. We could have kept tabs on your grades throughout."

Sarah reacted more acutely: in tears! "You don't understand! I'm trying to get into the pre-Pharm program. You gave me a 3.2; I needed at least a 3.5 in this class. I worked really, really hard this quarter! I spent some nights up till two a.m. You have to give me those other points!"

I repeated myself: "Sarah, we needed to have this conversation on *the first day*, especially with such high stakes for you. Also, time on the assignments doesn't automatically mean a high grade. There were some critical areas that were missed, and a lot of reading, which brought the grade down."

Then Sarah blew me away. "I showed up in class all the time! Doesn't that count? I'll do anything," she cried. "I'll mow your lawn. I'll babysit your kids."

Ugh. Bribery. Bribery has no place in communication between a student and a professor.

"Sarah, I get that you are feeling desperate right now," I said. "But what you are proposing is unethical, unprofessional, and not something that a professor would or should ever accept. If we continue this dialogue, I'm going to have to bring my division chair in."

Wide-eyed and red-faced, Sarah shook her head, "No, no. I'm very sorry. I am just very upset."

The Backstory

Grades are critically important. I felt the same way as a student. Grades get you that much closer to your degree. Given that, I'll cover this huge topic of how your grades happen over two chapters. You'll find tips for dealing with a grade dispute in a separate chapter toward the end of this book.

Back to the students, who I showcased above: I empathize with them. I know that feeling of desperation when you didn't plan for something, or you thought you were cranking out good work, and then you feel blindsided by the outcome. However, in every example, early planning and increased dialogue could have changed the outcome.

So what should you do? Take responsibility for the grade you "need" *on the first day or in the first week of the term.* Do *not* wait until midterm or finals time to figure it out. Otherwise, here's what you'll face:

Scenario 1: At midterm, you might decide to finally check your grades. You realize you aren't doing as well as you'd hoped. You panic. There are only three more assignments, the midterm, and the final left. A lot of pressure is riding on that work for a decent grade.

Scenario 2: You take your midterm exam and your grade is horrible. You've gotten good grades (low As, high Bs) until that point, but a bad headache kept you from doing your best on the exam. The exam is worth twice the points of those smaller assignments. Now you fear what will happen if you do okay on the remaining assignments but bomb the final.

Scenario 3: You reach the end of the quarter and finally pay attention to your grades. You add up your points and realize that your "goal grade" (i.e., A, B, C or even passing D), looks like it will not happen.

In all three situations, most students freak out, sirens blaring. They hunt me down for an appointment or send a frantic e-mail asking how to salvage the grade. What I hear is that *I* need to clean up the grade mess that the student caused by not starting this conversation far earlier. Some students will even blame me for not reaching their goals.

Let's talk about blame for a minute. Many students blame the prof because they "gave" a certain grade. Repeat this ten times: "Grades are earned, not given."

Profs don't play "grade bingo" or "grade darts" and arbitrarily hand you a grade. Any course syllabus includes a section called "Course Objectives" or "Outcomes." This is an academic way of saying, "Here's what I want my students to know or do at the end of this course." Sometimes your prof authors those objectives. Other times, a whole department, a committee, or an outside accrediting agency writes them. Objectives help your professor determine what to teach you and what your tests should be on. Then, your assignments, projects, exams, etc., determine how well you meet those objectives—in other words, how much you know about, or can perform, the subject matter. The letter or numerical grade from those assignments/tests tells your professor, and you, where you excelled and where your performance needed more work.

A lot of thought goes into assignments and tests. Some professors write these items from scratch; others use textbooks, instructor manuals, or borrow from other colleagues. We also get ideas from conferences we attend or organizations we belong to.

Some professors keep the same curriculum for years, and others change it every term. Some departments analyze every test question to see where students are struggling, then adjust the test. I am sharing this information so you can see the mental Olympics that go into choosing your classwork.

Even with these structured requirements and standards, grading is definitely the most crazy-complex, sometimes contentious part of a professor's job. Unless you haven't been told how you will be graded and given no requirements for assignments or exams, there shouldn't be blame for the grade you were "given."

In fact, I have a challenge for you: look inward and ask, "What could I have done differently to *earn* a better grade?"

Let's face it: if you start your ten-page research paper forty-eight hours before the deadline, then end up with a D because you wrote eight pages, then your actions "chose" that grade. Conversely, if you bust butt on that ten-page paper—researching like crazy, proofreading five times, even asking your professor to review—you earn an A, and you really *earned* it, right?

Let me address Sarah's "working hard" comment and her request for the professor to nudge her grade up .2 of a point. Many students believe that time on task automatically translates to a desired outcome.

I'm going to digress: I have always fought my weight. Morbid obesity is in my genes, and that stinks. In 1998, I went on an eleven-year journey to lose ninety pounds (I had two children in there). I counted calories, ran ten half-marathons, and did Zumba several nights a week. Even now, although I stopped running long distances, I go to CrossFit five mornings a week. In recent years, my weight has inched up. I gained back forty pounds; I'm still trying to figure out why.

Have I stopped taking care of my body? Absolutely not! As I update this book, in fact, my laptop is hoisted on a large cardboard box—a makeshift standup desk in my kitchen so I'm not so sedentary when not exercising. Am I still trying to figure out my calories? Of course! I have two apps on my phone.

So yes, I'm working "hard," but something is still off. Maybe age, hormones, stress, an incorrect balance of protein to carbs to fat—who knows? The bottom line is that hard work doesn't necessarily guarantee a particular result.

So back to you working "really hard" on classwork and thus earning a certain grade: there is just no guarantee. Your professor can't gauge how hard you worked until she sees your actual work. And time is subjective, isn't it? Some students perceive thirty minutes of studying as medal-worthy. Others think four hours is barely enough.

Let's not forget work *quality*. Time on task *and* meeting/exceeding the assignment requirements will hopefully produce a desired outcome, but if essential pieces are missed, then no amount of hard work will compensate.

I know that poor grades breed embarrassment. Students want to defend themselves by puffing up how much effort they expended. Professors can listen to your proclamation, but they can't factor your hard work into the grade outcome.

Which leads us to the final point before the talking tips in Part 2: your professor is not likely to bump your 3.2 to a 3.5 or anything else. If you have a 3.28, your professor *may* average you up to a 3.3. This depends on if he looks at "qualitative" elements of your performance in class (i.e., how much you contributed, if you had excellent attendance, etc.) or how close you really are to that next grade. But every professor handles this differently.

If you are asking for more of a nudge on your grade, realize that this "gift" equates to actual points in the class. Maybe a 10- or 25-point assignment. Should your professor hand you those points without you doing the work? How would that be ethical or fair to the rest of your class?

If you receive a grade that you feel is unfair or unclear, you have a right to take action. I'm going to tell you how in Chapter 32. But in the meanwhile, always look at *your* actions when it comes to grades. Did you sacrifice points on certain assignments because you skimped on the requirements or didn't understand them? Or maybe you worked on the assignment too late and didn't put in your best effort.

Regardless of the circumstances, I realize grades can come with an emotional charge. So let's focus on you confidently and competently navigating the conversations that surround them.

9. Your Grades, Part 2:

"Giving" Them, "Needing" Them, and Working "Hard" for Them

Ready for some smart talking regarding your grade issues? Here are your tips!

Ask Yourself This:

With respect to the grade you need:

When have I planned for other goals I've had? Trying out for a sport? For a job I wanted? For an item I had to save up to buy? Did I go to key people who could help me reach those goals and ask questions? What questions did I ask? What questions do I now realize I should have asked?"

When you feel that you've worked "hard" but didn't get what you wanted:

Why am I telling my professor how hard I worked on my test/studied for my assignment? Do I expect that my professor will raise my grade? Give me a chance to redo an assignment? Do I think that just because I worked hard, I should automatically receive a high grade, even if I didn't fully meet the requirements of the assignment or the test?"

When you feel that you've been "given" a grade:

Was I familiar with the assignment requirements ahead of time? Did I meet all of the requirements and check in with my prof to ensure that I was on the right track?

Think This:

I can talk to my prof about my grade goals early on in the term. If I don't start the discussion, I won't be able to develop a plan to reach my goal.

I am supposed to "work hard" in college. Much of the time, putting in a lot of quality study hours will result in the "reward" of high grades, but sometimes, I will work hard and I will not get the grades that I hope for or expect. I have to make sure that when I'm working "hard," I'm also meeting and exceeding the requirements.

If the assignment (exam, etc.) requirements were given to me ahead of time, and I didn't meet those requirements—or checked in to ensure that I was meeting them—then the grade I received is the one I earned. I need to take responsibility for that.

Not That:

> My professor owes me because I put in a lot of time
> on this assignment. I should get an A for my effort! I
> need an A so I can keep my GPA up.

There is no "WBO" (worked butt off) grade. Your prof has to grade you on something tangible: the requirements of the assignment and how well you mastered those requirements.

Say This:

About that grade you "need":

On the first day or in the first week:

> I'm trying to get into the nursing program and I have
> a goal of getting a 3.5 in this class. Do you have any
> advice to make that happen? Can I submit work
> early? If so, how early would you like me to submit
> my work so you will have time to give me feedback
> and I can work on what you tell me to? Are you
> willing to look at my work again after I apply your
> recommended changes? When should I check
> back with you to make sure my goal is on track?

Not That:

In the ninth or tenth week:

> But I needed a 4.0 in this class!

You should have thought ahead! Or, if the instructor is trying to help you reach your goal, never say:

That's too hard!

or

That's too much work!

Your credibility will be shot.

Say This

About working hard:

> I expected to receive a higher grade on this assignment. I started early and thought I met the full requirements. Where should I have spent more time?

Not That:

> I worked so hard. Can't you give me some credit for that?

You know the answer. No. The professor can't do that, even though he may be really, really, really (really!) impressed by your description of your effort.

Say This:

About that grade you believe you were "given":

> I am surprised and concerned about the grade I received. I was expecting it to be higher and believed I followed the requirements. Can you explain what needed to be done differently?

Not That:

> Why did you give me a C on this? I should have at least had a B!

Keep reminding yourself that your grade was calculated based on established standards and requirements. If you were unclear on those standards and requirements, request help well before the assignment is due.

The End Note

If your goal at school, work, in sports—wherever—involves another person, then both parties should share an *early* discussion about what is required to meet that goal. Think of an experience when your performance was evaluated: maybe you've been in sports, band, or you've done art or technology projects that were "judged." What if you received no guidance or direction to reach your goals but then found out what you could have done after the fact? Sounds crazy, right?

If you don't have an early conversation with your professor about how to meet your grade goals, you set yourself up for the real possibility that you won't meet those goals. Once you have the talk, you still have to do work that meets (and, ideally, exceeds!) the requirements to fit the grade you want. Your initial intention statement that you have a grade goal will set the tone for a consistent feedback loop with your professor. You'll partner with your professor every step of the way. Best of all, you will not become blindsided by a random grade. You won't even have to resort to bribery.

One last note, and hopefully one of comfort when you have that grade conversation: your goal doesn't have to be a 4.0. Professors know that students' goals vary. Some students seek the highest grades to attain and maintain scholarships. Other students are happy to pass with a very midline grade. No judgment! Your goals are personal to you and your experience, but whatever it is, go after it. Don't wait until the grade happens to you. Don't think that you're doing 4.0 or 3.0-worthy work only to find out later that it is 2.0 work and barely that.

And once you start trying to reach those goals, remember that in professional life, an employee can't just say, "I work hard." Any worker has to put effort behind those words. Really, the only time an employee can use verbal examples of how hard they work is during the initial interview: "I did a project in three weeks and submitted it ahead of deadline." After that, it's all about showing what you can do. No "credit"—promotion or raise—will come from the declaration that you worked "hard."

You'll get the good career stuff because you have a proven track record: those deliverables that back up your solid work ethic.

You know—your hard work!

The Career Note

For this interview, I sought out an industry expert who happens to be former faculty. He has made the shift from evaluating grades to evaluating job performance. Since grading is such a complex topic, I formatted this section a bit differently and asked myriad questions.

What mental shifts do students need to make to realize that they earn a particular performance rating based on their performance?

> One major shift is a different balance of personal and professional expectations that don't exist as clearly in an educational environment. In school, you obviously pick your major and your courses based

on your interests and how they help you reach your goals for graduation. As an employee, you need to clearly understand what a company expects from you and how they measure success so you can focus your attention on the efforts that have the greatest impact on that evaluation. Ideally, your personal goals should align with the goals of your position, but that isn't always as constant as it is when you are a student. Understanding the performance rating criteria at your job is crucial for success. I am amazed how few job applicants ask, "How will my performance be assessed in this position?"

Similarly, what should students realize about spending a lot of time on a project at work but not making sure they are on the right track throughout?

As an educator, I tried to teach my students to understand that time spent does not always equal quality. Working hard on something that is headed in the wrong direction is a frustrating waste of time. Assignments should clearly identify the audience for the material and ideally spell out risks to avoid. There are more practical matters in the workplace that help facilitate that structure. One benefit of a workplace environment is budget constraints. Most projects have budget targets and gates to assess how things are going. Client check-ins and tight deadlines help keep the focus on the final deliverable within a profit margin for the company. At the university level, students are expected to be more self-driven without daily exposure to a collaborative work environment. The students who were the most successful in my courses were the ones who came to office hours to touch base on projects along the way. That mirrors the work environment, where you have access to your project lead or your manager on a daily basis and you can check in for regular feedback on your work.

Finally, students are recommended to discuss grade goals/concerns during the first week of the term. When should an employee who is seeking a particular performance rating, promotion, or raise discuss these goals?

Many employers have regularly scheduled performance reviews where you can check in on how you are doing and where you are in the promotion cycle. One key aspect of understanding the expectations of your position is to understand if there is a range within that position that is rewarded financially and then a clear change of expectations when you advance to a more senior position. If you start to feel that you are performing at the higher end of your position's range or taking on duties that fall into the definition of a more senior role, then you need to discuss this with your manager. It is also important to know any timing expectations your company has around promotion. It can be a mistake to discuss raises and promotions too early in your tenure at a company. I have seen employees, too eager to advance, overstate their value and derail their careers. That being said, smaller companies may require you to have a more open dialogue about your career, as these organized management structures often don't exist.

Stephen, advertising/design

10. Passing the Course after Absences

What You Might Say:

I know I've been gone a lot. Can I still pass this class?

What Your Professor Thinks:

You haven't shown up for three weeks. We should discuss this.

The Real Story

Madelyn attended class regularly until her work schedule changed. Then she missed three weeks, but I had no idea why. She ultimately returned because she was laid off from her job.

Then the inevitable question: "Can I still pass?"

Then there was Parris, a steady attendee until his mother was diagnosed with cancer. Parris would take his mother to treatment, which would mean at least four missed classes.

With a strong GPA, Parris was worried. He asked, "Is there any way I can stay in this class?" Given the circumstances, Parris no longer cared about acing the class, just finishing.

The Backstory

Life happens in college. I know because it happened to me. When I was twenty-one, my father unexpectedly died. I stopped going to class during finals. I didn't talk to professors about options. I just faded away. Unfortunately, it took me six years to return to college. Not what I expected. Hence, I can relate to when students fall into a life situation and fall out of school.

Students who don't withdraw show up on my roster for the whole term. I can't withdraw the student after the first week, so if they don't do it themselves, I have to input a 0.0 grade—essentially an F. I hate to lose students when there was a situation we probably could have worked out.

I know that many students today are maxed out, juggling a job or two, have family responsibilities, etc. College may be the last thing on your mind when you can barely slog through another day. Or maybe you've chosen to skip a lot of class. Either way, you have to ask yourself, "Am I prepared to drop this class by the required date to avoid an F on my transcript?"

If the answer is "no" or even "I can't make the decision right now," contact your professor and see about options. He can help you make the decision.

Keep in mind that you are 100 percent responsible for seeing if you can salvage your class. I recommend this step whether you've missed class or you know you will miss more than a couple of class sessions in the future.

Before you meet with your professor, check out the syllabus attendance policy. Calculate worst- and best-case scenarios. See if you can stomach the grade outcome. Granted, your professor may not penalize you, but you can't count on that. Know the policy and its ramifications, then feel relief if the professor offers something else.

Your next step is to see what you've missed (or will miss), either by looking at the class schedule or talking to a classmate. Remember; take these actions *before* meeting your professor. You need to approach with a strategy rather than asking him to create a plan for you.

Let me reiterate: *you have a much better chance of saving the situation if you develop a proposal to show your professor rather than expecting him to do reactive crisis management.*

When you meet with your professor, don't share personal information if you feel uncomfortable. Honestly, the reasons why you were or will be out don't matter. I'm not saying your professor doesn't care. Most professors care very much. But your professor needs to ponder a solution. Your time is better spent laying out your proposal to stay in the class.

Make a dedicated appointment for this meeting. Be up front about its subject matter: you want to discuss your options to stay in the course or withdraw. If you withdraw, sure, you don't need this meeting, but think about it: you might end up with this professor again. He'll have more respect for you if he knows you didn't just bail out.

Another angle: some students miss class and never plan to return. Believe it or not, some professors may attempt to contact you (some professors won't—they are too worried about a FERPA violation, or they figure you have good reason). Don't worry: under FERPA law, a professor cannot ask or answer questions of anyone but you. I typically do not call missing students, but I will e-mail them, and many professors choose this route, too.

If your professor contacts you, don't avoid the conversation out of embarrassment. Say that some things happened and you appreciate him getting in touch. You never know what your professor might suggest to help the situation. Take the courtesy of his reaching out in the intended spirit.

Ask Yourself This

Do I have a history of missing class and then scrambling or quitting? How does this make me feel? Stressed? Ashamed? What stops me from getting help so I can get myself back on track?

Think This

If a life situation happens, I should talk to my professor immediately. I shouldn't make decisions without exploring options. The professor has dealt with these situations before and isn't there to judge me for missing class. The professor is there to help me figure this out.

Not That:

It won't matter if I talk to my professor. She will be mad because I've missed so much class.

Your professor has no reason to be mad. It isn't like your absences are personal, and if by some chance they are, then skipping class does more harm to you than to your professor.

or

I can take the penalty and catch up.

Many students overestimate what it takes to bring themselves up to speed and catch up on a bunch of work. Your professor will not revisit the material for you.

Say This:

The moment you know you'll have to miss classes, say:

> I'm going through something unexpected. I'm going to miss some classes (be specific, if possible), but I'm committed to finishing. I've looked at the schedule. I see you're covering X chapters. I can work through those myself. I realize there will be a penalty for my absences. I've calculated that even if I score low points for the remaining assignments, I can still get a C. Am I taking everything into consideration, given my circumstances? Do you have further advice for me?

(If your return is delayed, make sure you let your professor know how you plan to stay on top of that).

Here's another option if you are early enough in the term:

> Could I switch to another format for this course, such as online or hybrid?

I've seen students find relief from a rigorous on-campus schedule when moving to online or part-online format. See if this will work for you.

If you've already missed a lot of class, say:

> I missed a lot of class. I don't plan to miss further classes, and I hope to finish. I realize I should have gotten in touch with you sooner. I know I'll probably end up with a lower grade than I wanted. I looked at the syllabus and see that I've missed x chapters. I will go over those myself. Will you accept specific questions if I have them?
>
> Also, I reviewed the syllabus and see that my absences will cost me x points. If my calculations are correct, even with low grades on the remaining assignments, I can still get a C out of this class. Can you confirm that I am looking at this situation correctly? I appreciate your willingness to work with me, and I realize I should have gotten in touch sooner.

Caution: your professor can't insist that you drop the class, but he can tell you if your plan is flawed. You'll have to consider if you're willing to fight to salvage the class or if you should take it another time.

Not That:

> Can I still pass this class?

Acknowledge you've missed class before asking this and figure out for yourself if you can still pass.

or

> Can you just not ding me for being absent?

The professor has to do that for everyone if he does it for you.

or

> I have a note proving I was in the hospital (or your grandmother died, etc.).

Most professors don't recognize excused versus unexcused absences; she doesn't want to determine if your ill aunt is more excusable than another student's doctor's appointment. Unless your professor says you need a note, don't worry about it.

The End Note

Two types of absences that I didn't mention, but should: a) missing the very first day of class; and b) missing class on the day that something is due. Many students tell me that their planes didn't land on time, they didn't know when the first day of the term was, or they needed class time to finish an assignment.

Even just a few absences matter, particularly if those few are on strategic days (i.e., the first day of class or a due date). Realize that absences send a message about work ethic—a pretty loud message. What do you want others to perceive about you? Do you want to be seen as someone who shows up and is present, or someone who is intermittently gone without good reason?

If your absence(s) will cost you a grade, think about the long-term outcome of that. An F can weigh down your transcript until you retake the course or find a way to strike the F. This happened to me after my dad's death. At the least, try to get a C or D. You can average up those grades with a high GPA elsewhere. Even withdrawing from the class is better than failing.

As a professor, I want to say, "Go to class no matter what." And truth be told, your presence in the classroom is important. The learning community depends on you, whether you realize it or not. Yes, even if you don't say a word. Your presence *matters.*

I understand that absences are not always planned. I'm going to sound like a parent for a second: do better than I did when my father died. Be open with your professor about absences. Take responsibility for them and work out your own plan. Then be more mindful about your presence in the future.

The Career Note

With respect to absences in the workplace, my industry interviewee had a particularly relevant situation to share:

> *I have had an issue with absences in work study students. One in particular, seemed to miss more days the longer he had worked for me. Sometimes he would send an e-mail saying he was sick on the morning he was supposed to show up. However, the more of these I received, the less I believed him. This student was eventually terminated but didn't have the courtesy to show up for his scheduled exit interview and to close out his project.*
>
> *If an employee perpetually misses work on important days, such as when a project is due, I would want that person to know that their absence really impacts our workplace. I need to take my time and attention away from other tasks to complete the ones that that the person didn't do.*
>
> *If my employee missed the first day of work, unless this employee had a very good reason and*

contacted me well before he/she was scheduled to arrive, missing the first day of work would sour my opinion of his/her work ethic. I haven't had this happen per se, but I have been trying to find other work study students, and one just missed their interview without sending a reason or apology.

Jennifer, genetic research

11. Handling a Redo/ Receiving Feedback

What You Might Think:

Phew. Professor Hero is letting me redo that paper. I have more time.

or

Yeah, I have a bunch of comments on that paper. I don't have time to add anything else.

What Your Professor Thinks:

I don't have to give second chances. I also don't have to offer feedback on how to improve your work. Treat these opportunities like the gifts they are: gifts that can help you do better in my class.

The Real Story

Liam submitted a speech recording for my online class. He read the entire speech from a sheet of paper—no eye contact with the camera, no interaction with the audience, totally monotone voice.

Let's face it: anyone can read from a piece of paper. Learning how to interact with an audience requires a different set of skills. Speeches that are read verbatim earn an automatic zero for a grade. I know this sounds harsh, but when I say, "Create speaker's notes," there is no clearer way I can send that message.

In many cases, I will allow the student to rerecord their speech. It's a huge risk on my part. Students who did things right the first time would probably think: *Wow, this dude got a big break. Don't I deserve the chance to up my grade?*

I can see why you'd think this, but believe me, rerecording speeches is a total pain in the ass. Students have to gather an audience all over again and deliver a speech that they've probably mentally cast away. In Liam's case, he was really starting over again. He had to teach himself how to write speaker's notes for a speech that would now be late, then figure out how to actually make eye contact with an audience. See? Not easy.

In return for the second chance, my expectation is that Liam is going to say, "Thank you. I'll have this back to you within forty-eight hours" (or whatever date we mutually set). He won't wait weeks and weeks to submit. Liam will also check and see when the next assignments are due so he doesn't fall behind on those deadlines.

When Liam submits his revised speech, he won't insist that I grade it immediately. Instead, he will review the policy in my syllabus that says, "Late work does not get priority grading over a) on-time work that I'm reviewing before a major assignment; or b) major assignments already submitted on time." He will move swiftly to work on the next assignment and will definitely not repeat the same issue in the next speech submission.

Now let's say that Liam had a totally different issue. Let's say that he submitted his outline prior to his speech (which actually is how the progression goes in my class), and I gave substantial feedback for ways to improve the content for the actual presentation. What if Liam didn't take any of that feedback? What if he then presented a speech based on an outline with known problems?

A second chance is a pretty big bonus. Feedback that can create a stronger outcome for a subsequent assignment is an equally big bonus. I want you to treat both with a great deal of care!

The Backstory

I'll start by covering the "do-over" opportunity. The ideal progression for a do-over is for students to rapidly revise their work and resubmit it. Some students, however, will take their time. They may even submit the revised assignment after a future assignment is due, which prevents them from using feedback I might have provided. Then I have to slap a grade on the late assignment and call it a day. The feedback won't really matter.

There is one other scenario. The worst, really. Some students may ignore the redo offer and just take a zero. You've already read my feelings about taking a zero in the previous chapter.

Any way you slice it, a do-over is complicated. A professor risks other students finding out that someone else got to revise, so the students might think they'll have that opportunity as well and not try as hard on the first submission. So just because you hear that someone was able to redo work, don't automatically slack and think you can, too. Only the professor and that student know the circumstances behind the generous offer.

Also, professors pay heavily for do-overs in their time. Think about it: with Liam, I reviewed his recording, which took however many minutes. Then there were the back-and-forth e-mails to discuss the recording problems and the subsequent revision terms. And, because I offered the do-over, I'm going to grade his work again. In reality, I'm spending double the time on Liam's grade than I will on any other student—all because he didn't get his speech right the first time and I allowed him a do-over!

Many professors would say, "Idiot, you brought all this on yourself. You should just give him a zero and then he'll learn." I accept the ramifications for my decision to let my students redo work, and other faculty in this predicament do as well. Hence, if you get the opportunity to revise your work, take the gift you're being offered. Ignoring the opportunity just makes you look discourteous and unprofessional. Waiting to complete the work increases the chance that you will get bogged down by other assignments, life, etc. Finally, the quality of your resubmission obviously needs to be higher than what you turned in the first time. You'll be most motivated if you start when the information is fresh in your mind.

Submit your work on the date that you and your professor agreed to, and then move forward. Don't pester your professor to get your grade back to you. She can't grade your late/revised work before other students' on-time assignments. And, really, she has no obligation to give you a time frame. Just be thankful for the opportunity.

Let's shift to Liam's other hypothetical situation: he received feedback prior to delivering his speech, and he didn't take it. Giving and receiving feedback is going to be one of the biggest parts of your professional life. If someone is grading or evaluating you and they give you things to work on but you ignore those things, then that inaction will speak very loudly, and not in a positive way. Also, remember that if you are receiving feedback, the person giving you the suggestions likely wants you to improve. And think about it, your professor has nothing to gain or lose if you raise your grade or not. You might as well take the advice and use it to make your work stronger!

Ask Yourself This:

What prevented me from meeting the requirements the first time? Did I need additional help? Am I willing to get help next time, rather than spend extra time redoing my work?

Think This:

Redoing work takes double the time. I'm better off knowing what to do from the start and doing my best on that.

Not That:

It doesn't matter how I do on this assignment. I can either redo it, or I'll just take a zero.

Your professor may not allow a redo, and a zero can bring your GPA down.

Say This:

If a redo is not offered to you, ask:

I realize that I didn't do my best on the first attempt for this assignment. I believe I could do better. Is there any way that I can redo it for partial credit?

If your professor says "yes," then ask:

> When would you like me to resubmit my work? Can you give me an idea of how the points will work, since it's a redo?

You can go on to say:

> I realize you will be grading other assignments first, but should I expect to use the feedback from this assignment for the next one?

If your professor says "no," don't push it. Instead, you can say:

> I want to make sure I don't make this mistake again. When should I meet with you to get help for the next assignment and make sure I'm on track? Will you review that work early for me? How will this grade affect my overall grade?

Not That:

> You have to give me another chance! This isn't fair! I didn't understand what I was supposed to do! I know I can do better next time!

If your professor is not allowing a do-over, there is likely a very good reason. There will be little that you can say to change his/her mind, so move forward to the next assignment and try to strengthen your grades as much as you can.

The End Note

Quick story: I received my first column advancement (think raise in pay), an opportunity which only comes every three years. During this process, I submit a portfolio of my achievements, the portfolio is evaluated, and then I either receive the raise or I don't. I did receive the raise, and in the e-mail, my vice president said he had a few other suggestions for my next packet submission (yes, in three years) and the door was open if I wanted to meet to go over them. Think about if I ignored my boss's opportunity. What if I just said to myself, "Well, I passed and that's what's important!"? I'm sure this would not reflect well on me at all. As it turned out, I did meet with the VP, wrote down his suggestions, and, after three years had passed, I was able to resubmit another strong packet which reflected his input.

In this example, if my packet wasn't solid the first time around, there would be no do-overs. I simply wouldn't get the raise, and I'd have to wait three more years. The same could be said if I ignored the feedback I was given.

Be savvy when given tangible suggestions to improve. The rewards may be a higher grade, an increase in pay, or just the idea that someone cares enough to see you want to do better.

The Career Note

I wondered what the ramifications are for not responding to feedback in the workplace. I wanted to know what would happen if feedback was ignored:

> In the healthcare field, I think it is particularly important to welcome the suggestions of my colleagues. For example, an ailing patient may have a fickle personality—volatile one moment, serene the next. This is not unusual when body chemistry is altered.

If a colleague approaches to help me connect to a patient, I should not shy away from it. Rather, I should arm myself with the information and utilize it to see if my strategy improves.

Medical personnel, in my opinion, should instinctually adhere to the suggestions of their supervisors. The health of patients often depends on it. Our supervisors generally have experience and knowledge that surpasses our own. Supervising staff at the home health company where I work recently suggested a more rigid approach to ensuring patient compliance; this meant electronically checking each patient's data on a weekly basis. Some practitioners accepted this suggestion, while others felt that the current strategies were fine and chose not to accept the new ones. Ultimately, those who made the change had patients who were more compliant and with better health scores overall.

Criticism doesn't always equate to negativity, though many have a difficult time accepting criticism, even when positive. Accepting suggestions breeds broader perspective and, in a professional workplace, supervisors and coworkers can offer a world of insight and tools that can be useful.

Angelee, respiratory care

---

12. Extra Credit

My grade is too low. Can I do some extra credit?

What Your Professor Thinks:

Extra credit shouldn't be expected to save your grade.

The Real Story

Angelo missed a required journal assignment which was worth 100 points. Hoping to improve his overall grade, he asked, "Can I do some extra credit to make up for this?"

I know very few professors who would offer 100 points of extra credit. Five points, 25 points, maybe 50 points, but 100 points? No.

Let's say Angelo receives extra-credit work worth 20 points (if I offered extra credit at all, that would be my average). Angelo will spend his time doing—more work. He still has yet *more* work because there are upcoming assignments. I suppose you could argue that Angelo "saved" time because he didn't do his journal assignment. But now, he has some extra writing which won't even yield him enough to overcome 100 lost points. Angelo would have been better off turning in part of the journal assignment. Even a failing grade would be 50 points, which is more than he'll earn with extra credit!

Here's another example: Marjorie received a C on one of her speeches due to lack of quality sources. Like Angelo, Marjorie asked about extra credit so she could nudge her C to a B. Now Marjorie will spend time doing extra credit when she could have used her time securing excellent sources for her speech. Not to mention that she had another speech coming up in three weeks which would also require research time.

Let's look at one final student: Tyler had an A. He didn't need extra credit, but he wanted the insurance policy. Based on Tyler's performance, there was no doubt in my mind that he'd end up with an A. But if I offered him extra credit, his attention would divert from his A-level effort in my class—or even in his other classes. I wanted him to stay focused on the great work he was already doing!

The Backstory

I already know that my position about extra credit is unpopular, but I think it's a colossal waste of time. The only students who seek extra credit are often the ones who don't need it or the ones who can't benefit from it enough to make a tangible grade difference.

I know you are going to say that there are some professors who make extra credit really worth it, but I'll still argue that extra work is just that: extra. Instead, make your time work for you. Get your assignments done early. Ask for an early review from your professor (see Chapter 18), and that's your extra credit right there. Getting early feedback and the chance to achieve a stronger grade on work you already have to do is the insurance policy to strive for the grade you want. You'll never need extra credit with that approach. I'd so much rather students spend their precious study time working early on assignments and letting me check them rather than doing subpar work and then using extra credit as a fix on the back end.

Think about it: if your overall grade tanks, then only a ton of extra credit will save an entire term's poor grades. I don't know many professors (or *any* professors) who would offer that much extra credit.

All this said, there is one time that extra credit might make sense: if you are taking a class where your entire grade hinges on a series of examinations and quizzes and there is *no* other way to show what you know, you may need to request extra credit. We all know that not everyone tests well. An exam is a snapshot of someone's knowledge at a single moment in time. It is not typically a work in progress, like, say, a research paper or a speech or even homework that consists of increasingly challenging mathematical equations.

Without getting into a lot of boring educational theory, if your grade is built solely on quizzes and examinations, that grade may not tell the whole story. A student should receive a grade based on different ways to show knowledge, but not every professor feels that way. If you have one of these professors and your tests aren't going well, you may need to ask for extra credit.

The extra credit could take the form of you going back to your incorrect test questions and writing up some brief explanation about why you missed those items and what you now know about them. This will require more work and research on your part, but guess what? You will actually *know* the material, which is likely your professor's goal, rather than cramming the information just to do well on the test and forgetting that information shortly thereafter.

I'm not saying that your professor will offer extra credit in a situation like this, but you could ask. It would probably go over better than telling your professor that his means of measuring your knowledge is flawed because he is using a single method (all tests) to do so. On the professor's side, giving you some extra credit is easier than revamping an entire curriculum that may have been in use for years and years.

Don't get me wrong: I still believe that extra credit is a more negative than positive component of education. In the work world, an employee can't do a terrible job and then suddenly ask what extra work she can do in order to get a better review or raise. Evaluation happens consistently during the employee's day-to-day performance, not in a "save your ass" moment when you suddenly decided to rise above.

Another thing to consider is that, if you are granted extra credit, what if the work isn't really worth the points? What if it's work you don't want to do? If you're miserable doing the extra credit or you aren't learning anything from it because it's really busywork, then the few points you will get won't feel like any sort of win.

Ask Yourself This:

Do I often ask for extra credit to bring my grades up? What is preventing me from achieving the strongest grades on the work that is already required? Am I devoting enough time to that work? Do I need additional help? Am I asking for my work to be reviewed early?

Think This:

Extra credit won't be needed if I perform to the right standards on work I already have to do. My professor can help me figure out what those standards are.

Not That:

I don't have to do well on this assignment. I'll just ask for some extra credit to bring my grade up.

Remember, not every professor offers extra credit, some extra credit isn't enough to make a substantial difference, and you are going to take time away from assignments that are still due or work in other classes.

Say This:

I was looking over my grade and see that I'm very close to getting an A (or whatever your next grade threshold is). I'd really like to make that happen. Do you have some advice about the assignments that are still due so I can earn as many points as possible? Will you take a look at some of my work early? When should I get that to you?

If you are hell-bent on doing extra credit but there are more assignments to come, say:

My grade isn't quite where I was hoping it would be. I am wondering if there is extra credit available. I would be glad to either take another look at the work I've already done or do an additional assignment. I will get more help on the assignments coming up so this doesn't happen again.

If nothing else is due and your overall grade is low, say:

I realize that I should have done things differently this term. I have a much lower grade than I was hoping. I'd like to bring it up, even a little bit. Do you offer extra credit, and would it help my average?

If your class falls into the "all quiz/exam" scenario I mentioned earlier, say:

I did not do very well on my quizzes/exams, and my grade is low. I am concerned that I know more about this material than what the test scores show. Is there anything I can do to raise this grade?

Note that you aren't asking directly for extra credit, but if your professor offers you an option to *raise* the grade, extra credit is essentially what you'll be getting. If possible, show your professor any other type of work that backs your claim about knowing the material.

Not That:

Why can't I just do extra credit to bring up my grade?

Extra credit is a privilege and a benefit; your professor is never obligated or required to offer it. Your professor *is* obligated to help you do your best on the required assignments as long as you are putting in equal effort.

The End Note

One of my favorite college/high school success authors and popular *Study Hacks* blogger, Cal Newport, has a mantra: "Work smarter, not harder." Remember this when you consider extra credit to raise your grade. Sure, the additional points could help you, but the time and the effort will take something away from you. All of your time is important, so be selfish. Get the most out of the work that you have to do, and then you won't have to do extra work.

The Career Note

For this topic, I had a fairly simple question: If an employee is doing a poor job to begin with or not meeting expectations, can a sudden burst of extra work help their standing? The author of *Forget Job Security: Build Your Marketability!* had this to say:

> *Unfortunately, in the work world, there usually aren't any "do-over" or extra-credit opportunities. If you aren't performing well, employers raise an eyebrow and start scrutinizing your work. If you continue to underperform, your job is at risk, and there isn't a lot you can do to rescue the situation. If you are lucky, you'll have a compassionate supervisor who will take the time to sit down one-on-one with you to find out what the obstacles are and work with you to overcome them. But business moves forward, and the corporate world does too, unrelentingly so. That*

means that employees are expendable. If you don't work out, there is usually someone else who is waiting to fill your shoes who can do the job. The key to success is to be willing and not afraid to reach out if you get in over your head. If you don't tell them you need help, then they don't know how to provide it. Communication is key. You are not a failure by asking for assistance before things go off the rails; instead, by asking for help, you are taking a proactive approach in managing your career before it is too late.

Dawn, career consultant

---

13. Finding Out What's on the Test

What You Might Say:

Will this be on the test?

What Your Professor Thinks:

Is what you're learning only important if it's on a test?

The Real Story

My students and I do a crazy class activity that involves personal space. Students pair up and we head outside (if the weather is decent). Students walk eight to ten feet away from each other and carry on a conversation. Then, students progressively step in closer and closer until their toes are touching, all while maintaining this conversation. Discomfort ensues; personal "bubbles" are invaded, which is the whole point. When we're finished, we discuss Edward T. Hall's theory of proxemics (nonverbal messages about space).

Now, the magic question that many students want to know: "Will this be on the test?"

The answer? No, it's not. The activity is designed to illustrate our individual reactions to "space invasion" as it relates to non-verbal communication. Then, my students will identify why they feel uncomfortable when someone is too close or, conversely, when someone they love is creating physical distance.

Now for the conundrum: Will my students pay attention if this material isn't on a test? Will they involve themselves in the activity/discussion as thoroughly?

I, too, wanted to know what was on the test when I was a student. But as a professor, I am sad that students lose meaningful moments as they wrestle with what information is attention worthy—or just "test worthy."

The Backstory

Your professors want you to love learning for the sake of learning. That's pretty flowery, I know. We wish you could let go of what will/won't be on the test because that sends the message that you view everything else as throwaway. Our goal is for you to become a keen critical thinker, one who is worldly, knowing—educated!

Of course, you want to be competitive for your career, and the bottom line is that you need grades that lead to a college degree for that career. So it's understandable that you want to pinpoint *the exact material* to focus on so you can study your little heart out and ace your tests. Unfortunately, many professors just won't feed you information only so you can score high on exams.

Think about it: What would you gain if the professor said, "Okay, pages 22, 25, 46, 53, 63, 77, 79-84, 90, 92, 94-98, and 102. That's on your test!"?

What would be the point of coming to class? Of being in a classroom with other intellectual people? What would be the point of your entire college education?

What would you be learning and enhancing within yourself if you just focused on the end result? Aren't you in college to expand yourself? (I'm not talking about the freshman fifteen).

There is a part of you that knows the answer is "yes"!

So, should your tests be a guessing game? Of course not, and I'll discuss that topic in Chapter 13. But there is a middle ground between being spoon-fed every test question and studying aimlessly for exams, hoping to land on the right content.

Remember when I discussed those course objectives back in Chapter 8? To recap, objectives are what you, the student, should be able to know/do at the end of the class.

Your test material should relate to those course objectives.

Look at your weekly learning material (units, modules, even chapters of your textbook). There will be "smaller" objectives there which, in tandem with the course objectives, will tell you what you'll likely be tested on.

If you see words like "demonstrate," "explain," or "apply," those objectives indicate that you'll *do something* with that information. It's a safe bet that those concepts could be on an assignment or test! How else will your professor know if you can "demonstrate," "explain," or "apply" without giving you the opportunity to do so, right?

Here's a quick example: one of the major course objectives for my Intro to Communication course is "Apply principles of cultural diversity to human/interpersonal communication, small group communication, and public speaking."

"Apply" means that students will "show" that they can do something. Therefore, there will be an assignment or test that covers some aspect of cultural diversity. In my course, students apply principles of cultural diversity in discussion forum questions, journal questions, and their major speeches. I don't test, but if we think of those major assignments the same way, then yes, that course objective gives students a huge clue about how they will be graded.

Here's a suggestion: next time you're in class, see if that day's content matches up to some of those course objectives (or the unit/chapter objectives). Then you'll know if you should start to formulate a study guide for an upcoming test—whether your professor gives you one or not (and remember that you need to be present when that study guide is handed out—or search for it in your course management system, if it is posted there).

You may be wondering, "Why do I have to be an academic brain surgeon? I can just ask my professor if that day's lesson is going to be on the test. Heck, I can ask my professor if his last sentence is going to be on the test!"

You could do this, but you'll annoy the hell out of your professor. Instead, care about all the material you're learning, regardless of whether or not it shows up on a test! With that attitude, you're going to benefit: you'll add to your "knowledge capital," and that's what you want to succeed!

Ask Yourself This:

Is my main goal to take and pass tests to get my grades, or do I view my classes as a way for me to broaden myself on the way to getting my degree? Do I believe I shouldn't have to study or even learn material that isn't on the test? Am I worried I'll be wasting my time, or am I concerned that I'll fail if I don't study the right content?

Think This:

I will probably find out what's on my tests because the professor will offer study guides or do a review in class. I do not need to constantly ask. If I am worried about studying the wrong information, there are other ways to find out.

Not That:

I don't want to do extra work. I just want to be ready for the test.

If you have that mindset, then you are expecting your professor to feed you test questions and answers, and anything outside of that will feel like "extra."

Go back to your syllabus or college catalog. Look at the title of your class. You are meant to get basic, intermediate, or advanced (depending on what the name of your class is) education on that topic. You may or may not be tested, but your professor has prepared ten to fifteen weeks of learning for you. He doesn't consider that "extra" at all.

Say This:

If your professor hasn't provided a test study guide, say this at least two to three weeks before the exam (preferably at the beginning of the term):

Professor, I see that we have a couple of major tests coming up. I will be working on my own study guides, but I am also wondering if you will be giving us something as well or having a review session in class.

Still worried that you aren't studying the right material for the test? Here's what to do:

First, have your professor's study guide in hand (if he gave you one). This document should have some of your own notes on the side, and you should have a study guide that you also created (essentially, to show that you've done something with it yourself).

This document could be mapped with the objectives that I told you about earlier. For example, if you have a midterm, then you would look at any objectives that would reflect what you should know/do to that point in the term. Then go to your professor and say:

> Professor, I've been studying this for the exam and just want to be sure that I'm focusing on the right concepts. I made my own notes and even looked at some of the objectives to see what I should know at this point. Can you check my list of topics and make sure I'm reviewing the right information? I'd like to do as well as I can on this test. I'm trying to ace it, if possible.

Just the idea that you would a) create your own study guide and b) try to do something with those course objectives is very likely going to blow your professor's mind in a good way.

Not That:

> You know that lesson from yesterday? Is any of that going to be on the test? What about the day before? How about what we're doing tomorrow?

Your professor is going to know that you just want to be fed answers, that you aren't interested in learning the material (even if you are actually interested, your message isn't going to come across that way). Get answers by showing that you've taken action to help yourself first.

The End Note

You probably know by now that the advice I'm giving you is 100 percent designed to help you feel more confident and sound more competent in your interactions. Asking what will be on a test is like going into work every single day and asking your boss, "Will doing this task get me a raise?"

That would grate on your boss's nerves, just like the test question grates on your professor's nerves. And in a professional situation, showing that you only want to do work that will get you a promotion or more money is the exact opposite way to make those things happen.

Over and over again in this book, you'll see that the key to getting help and respect from your professor is to do your own work first and then come armed with a plan, proposal, or an attempt. Then the questions you do ask will be taken seriously.

And chances are, you'll be so on top of things that others will come to *you* wondering what's on the test!

The Career Note

The workplace version of "Is that going to be on the test?" translates into an employee only doing work they believe will keep them above the radar or only seeking the "important" tasks that will elevate their standing, rather than the less enjoyable grunt work. I reached out to a career expert who blogs at *Recruitinginferno.com* to find out how these behaviors would be perceived:

I'm pretty sure early careerists don't realize that while college is more about them, the workplace is more about them and the team—your weights may vary. So in addition to asking managers questions pertaining to your work, one specific question needs to be directed towards those on your team: How can I help you? Being nice, sincere, and honest bodes well—not only for your performance, but also for the performance of the team. And yes, it does sound like lessons learned in kindergarten. Remember, while you've had four years to learn the politics of academia, you have far less time to learn the mazes, quicksands, dead ends and politics of work. Your professors, career services, and even recruiters will likely not tell you about your group's and company's Good, Bad, and Ugly. "Yesterday we were recruiting you but today you're staff" is not only the punchline of a recruiting joke but reality.

Steve, recruiting, talent, and social media consultant

---

14. Cheating/ Plagiarism

What You Might Think:

It's not that big a deal to copy/cheat/plagiarize. The professor won't even find out.

What Your Professor Thinks:

I've been at this a long time and am more attuned to cheating than you realize. The consequences for you can be pretty terrible.

The Real Story

Maylynn turned in speech content that included a quotation from the *Hoboken Reporter*. A regional newspaper is a perfectly credible source. The problem wasn't the information or the citation itself; the problem was that I recalled another student using the exact same source a year prior. Why would this be an issue? Because, sure enough, both students cited the same information for an almost identical speech topic. As I investigated further, I discovered that Maylynn had actually lifted whole segments of my former student's speech outline and passed it off as her own.

More recently, Anders submitted a paper with a very conversational introduction. The body of the paper had the "voice" of a research paper or textbook. Sure enough, the body of the paper was a research paper, one that was publicly available on a college blog.

Finally, let me share the tale of Trevor and Chris. Both submitted private journals in my interpersonal class, and each responded to one of the questions by discussing a miscommunication with a parent. Each student's story was almost identical. I had a hard time believing that Trevor and Chris experienced nearly the exact same heated argument with their father. They aren't brothers, just friends!

You probably realize that each of these situations constitutes cheating. And in every scenario here, the students admitted that they didn't think I would find out.

The Backstory

So how did I find out?

In Maylynn's case, she suffered from the fact that I have a good memory. A source like the *Hoboken Reporter* isn't used every day, so it's something that I would easily remember. Using the same source as another student is not an issue, but using the same written content is plagiarism!

Plagiarism is copying any other person's work, whether it's your friend or the content of an article, book, website, etc., and passing it off as your own. You probably already know that.

You may be wondering how I was able to locate the other student's paper to confirm the offense. That's actually pretty easy. Student work is submitted in a course management system. I have access to years of student assignments. I can pull any of them up at a given time. Now, if your professor doesn't use a course management system, don't assume you are in the clear. Work submitted via e-mail or other website can also be tracked. I am horrible at deleting files on my work PC or my home laptop. All I have to do is search my "downloads," and I can likely find things from years ago!

Anders's misstep was far easier to trace. All I had to do was copy the textbook-ish sounding sentences into my Google search box. Boom! Up came the research paper. Even if only a few words were changed, sophisticated Google will show me my search results, highlighting altered words from the original piece.

And let's not forget Trevor and Chris: even though they didn't copy an outside source, they copied each other. This is another form of cheating, and it's also plagiarism.

In all three of these situations, I held private meetings with the students. I had to reveal to them that I had proof of cheating. At my college, the consequences for cheating can be as minimal as a warning and a zero on the assignment or as grave as having a formal letter sent from the dean, a hearing, and possible expulsion from school. Cheating is very, very serious.

Never underestimate the ability of your professor to suspect and investigate cheating. If your professor is familiar with your writing and the tone suddenly doesn't match, that can be a red flag. If you were doing marginally or poorly on exams and then suddenly start acing everything, this can be a warning sign, too.

If you think that there are times when professors can't prove cheating, there is certainly truth to that. But why would you want to risk it? Why would you put your entire college education in jeopardy?

On many occasions in this book, you'll hear me recommend that you should be selfish. Selfish about your time management, selfish about getting the help you deserve, and selfish about using the college experience to benefit you in every way possible.

Cheating isn't the right use of selfishness. It's a cowardly shortcut, one that doesn't get you the real help you need and deserve and one that could ruin your entire college education. Is cheating really worth it when there are so many other options available to you? You could get additional help, you could talk to your professor about submitting a late assignment, or you could even turn in totally crappy work and probably get some points (which are better than nothing). See Chapter 18. All of those options aren't as risky as cheating.

Ask Yourself This

> *Why do I cheat? Do I have a habit of cheating? What risks am I willing to accept if I'm going to cheat? What would happen if I got help instead? Why am I not allowing myself to get the help that I need and deserve?*

Think This

> *If I'm cheating, I likely don't understand the work I have to do. I may copy someone else's assignment, and it could be wrong. I may copy work from an outside source, and my professor could definitely find out. I have to accept the risk that I likely will get caught, and even if I don't, I've cheated myself*

out of getting assistance that I'll probably need for other assignments in this class or another class.

Not That

I'll change the writing up so much that no one will ever know that I copied.

Think about it: if you're going to go to the trouble of changing someone else's writing, why not just spend that same amount of time writing your own fresh material?

or

The professor sucks, so I have the right to cheat.

The professor may suck. Cheating doesn't punish her for sucking, but it could punish you in a big way. There are things you can do to survive a crappy professor. There are fewer things you can do to save yourself after cheating.

Say This

If you haven't cheated yet but are tempted:

I am struggling to get through this assignment. I feel really frustrated. I got this far (explain what you've done already) and I really need advice on how to finish.

If you have cheated and you've gotten caught:

I made a mistake and I didn't consider the consequences ahead of time. Please explain what will happen next. Is there any way that I can make up for this error in judgment?

Like I said, some professors will let you off with a warning and a zero. Others will immediately report your actions to a dean of student services, disciplinary committee, etc., and the cheating will become an official part of your school record. If you have more than one offense, you will likely undergo a hearing and face being kicked out of school. Not worth it!

The End Note

I remember many times when I was a student and I struggled and felt totally desperate. In Chapter 34, I describe my environmental science class which infuriated me because I despised the boring professor and I couldn't get excited about the content. That entire class was all multiple-choice exams, so hating the professor and the content didn't do me any favors.

I knew a student who took the course before and still had those multiple-choice tests. Apparently, they never changed term to term. I figured if the professor was stupid enough to let that happen, then there was no reason I shouldn't take advantage.

You know what? Having those tests didn't help me one bit. I didn't find the content any more interesting when studying answers from tests that had already been completed. My conscience and sick guilt wouldn't allow me to even use the tests after the first one. I didn't get a good grade on that exam or any others.

That class was the one and only time that I ever attempted academic dishonesty. I taught myself a hard lesson, and I'm lucky that I didn't do permanent damage. I handled future difficult classes much differently: I talked to the professors, I hired my own tutors (thank you, teenage math whiz with a Mohawk who helped me get through college stats), and, sometimes, I simply accepted the grade that I deserved and just tried to average up elsewhere.

These days, cheating happens at least once every term, sometimes even a few times. Whenever I need to confront students about cheating, I get a sick twist in my stomach every time. The conversation is never easy, students are typically remorseful and embarrassed, and I have to make difficult decisions about the consequences. Let the student off with a warning, and that may not send a strong enough message. Allow a student to redo the assignment, and that's like a reward I can't give to everyone.

In my heart, I know that every case of cheating arises from confusion or desperation. I hope I can encourage you to channel your challenges in a way that will actually benefit you. Believe that you deserve not to deal with the havoc that a cheating offense can wreak on your personal and academic life.

The Career Note

I figured that in the workplace, cheating/plagiarism takes on the form of someone taking credit for someone else's work. I asked my interviewee if she's ever experienced this or someone who didn't get all their facts before making a suggestion:

> Yes, I worked with someone who would take credit for someone else's work, but in this particular workplace, we had a very observant manager who was in touch with his employees. His management style was hands-on; he always knew what was going on. In this particular situation, an employee made a mistake with a shipment, and it ended up being

labeled for one store when in reality it was an order for another store. Another employee figured out what happened and started taking steps needed to fix the error. The person who made the mistake became aware of the problem. He started changing paperwork and computer records to make it look like the man who found and fixed the problem was the one who actually made a mistake. Then the person who caused the problem looked like he was the one fixing it—at least in the records. Well, my manager knew better. He used redirection and very patient questioning methods without actually accusing him of it all. Eventually, the employee confessed to everything he had done. It needed to happen because the employee he was framing was already getting written up by higher management, and word was he was on the verge of getting fired. Instead, my manager fixed the problems, got the shipment out the door, and actually saved both jobs. The employee who caused all the issues actually did something similar a few months later and was terminated.

Ellie, shipping, retail

Managing Assignments/
Your Schedule

15. Figuring Out Textbooks

What You Might Say:

Do I really need to buy this textbook?

What Your Professor Thinks:

If the textbook is "required" in my syllabus, then it's required.

The Real Story

Tal ordered his textbook for my class from an online source. He told me that he couldn't complete the first assignment—due on the first week of class—because the book might take three weeks to arrive. Tal didn't realize he'd have homework so soon.

Louisa couldn't afford to buy the book because she was strapped for cash. She asked me if she could borrow one of mine or if I had a copy on loan at the library.

Like Tal, Parker purchased the text from an online source, but it was three editions out of date. He answered two journal questions incorrectly because he didn't double-check the current edition's chapter content with his older copy.

Did all these students create a major issue for themselves? Believe it or not, not entirely. Let's discuss …

The Backstory

Truth be told, many professors *and* students find textbooks stressful. Students pay $234 and then are understandably pissed when the book isn't used. Professors become frustrated when students don't turn in work or are unprepared because of a textbook problem. See? Stressful on all ends.

You may think, *My professor doesn't care. He doesn't have to pay the $234!* But a lot of professors are very sensitive to sky-rocketing book prices. Then there are professors who aren't as in touch with textbook costs and, of course, some who don't use the text anyway.

Asking your professor if she will actually use the book is a reasonable question, but it's one that may not get you the answer you're looking for. A well-meaning professor may say, "Yes, we'll use the book every day in class," and then change curriculum that doesn't require as much textbook use. Few professors would list a textbook and then say, "You know, I really don't use the book. Don't bother."

Try to look at this a different way: almost all professors assign readings, and those readings have to come from somewhere—either a textbook or articles, online sources, etc. My biggest recommendation to you is to look at your syllabus and see the required materials. If there is a textbook listed, assume you need it. You don't want to give the professor the idea that you are trying to take shortcuts.

Arrange to acquire your textbook nice and early. If you have several weeks before the class starts, your options for book buying widen. Your syllabus will tell you what books are required, but you may not have access to that document until the first day of class. You can go to the college bookstore; they are sure to have the information (by the way, you can find out what your books are from the bookstore even if you end up not buying the book there).

You can confirm the correct textbook by e-mailing the professor before the class starts or talking with a building secretary or even another professor in the department.

Next, figure out how you will get your textbook.

Will you go to the college bookstore, pay full price, and try to do a sell-back later?

Will you try to find a used copy at the bookstore so you can pay less? Will you order online?

Will you borrow an old copy from a friend? (If you choose this route, make sure that the copy is a current edition, or find out if you are permitted to use an old edition.)

Will you rent a textbook?

Will you share a book with another student in class?

Will you use a digital version?

Will you go to the library two hours every day and use the copy from the reference shelves? What if there isn't one on reserve? What if someone else has checked it out when you need it?

I realize that most college students want and need to save money, which is why they search for alternatives to buying textbooks. Out of fairness and respect for the service of college bookstores as well as the numerous options from publishers, I can't easily advocate one method of textbook acquisition over another. All of your choices have merit, although some may be more convenient than others (like having your own text rather than sharing) or hold more consequences (like the time you'd need to sit in the library "borrowing" the book or having to read a book in a way that isn't comfortable [i.e., on a device]). Instead, I will give you the questions to ask your professor so you can make the right decision for yourself.

Ask Yourself This:

Have I been caught unprepared without the right materials before? Has this caused me negative consequences in turning in work? Am I willing to potentially lose points (or credibility) if I don't have my textbook?

Think This:

I'll learn about what textbooks I need nice and early. Then I can figure out the smartest way to access/ acquire/pay for them.

Not That:

I'll go to class first and find out if I really need the book.

If the syllabus says that the textbook is required, it's required. Be in the "right" on this one. You never know if the professor is going to dive into course work or give you an assignment within the first forty-eight hours. Show a strong work ethic. Be prepared.

Here are different types of productive questions you can ask related to getting your textbook:

> The bookstore has X listed as the book you require for the course. I just want to make sure this is correct.

> I found a previous edition of X book that is a fraction of the price. Do you require students to have the most current edition of the book, or can we purchase an older copy?

Many professors will be perfectly fine with this, while others, due to the nature of their discipline's changing content, will require you to use the latest version.

> Do you know of other students from a previous term who might want to sell their textbooks?

Some professors facilitate these types of exchanges through a course management system. You never know.

Not That:

> Do we really need the text?

You already know my answer here.

> My book won't be here for three more weeks. Can I submit my assignments when it comes in?

I don't know many professors who would allow late work due to shipping issues with a textbook. If you did decide to order a textbook online and it won't be in for three weeks, ask if there are chapter outlines, PowerPoint or other presentation files, or lecture notes that you can use to still submit the assignment.

Note: even if your professor has comprehensive materials online that supplement your book, those materials are just a supplement. They aren't meant to replace the book. Beware of thinking that you can skip buying the textbook and just use the online materials. Also, figure out a backup strategy for yourself if your professor has no resources available to you until your book arrives. In that case, you'd have to share a book with another student, use the library, or possibly even try to rent a book for a short period of time.

> I am sharing a textbook with Shanna, and she has been absent the past two weeks. What should I do?

If you choose to share a book, then you are 100 percent responsible for the consequences if your partner takes sole custody. Your professor probably won't make an accommodation.

> Can I borrow a textbook from you or from the library?

If you have a very serious financial situation and you absolutely cannot buy a textbook, there is a chance that your professor will have a desk copy or two on hand. I keep a few books in my office for extreme situations. The professor may very well have put your book on reserve in the library, but you wouldn't be able to check it out. Most textbooks are only for use in the library for a period of time (say, two hours or so, depending on your library's policy).

The End Note

You might be surprised that I didn't say each of the students at the beginning of this chapter committed a major fault by ordering their text online, asking to borrow a textbook, or having an older edition. Professors know that students make tough choices when acquiring textbooks. As a professor, I'll tell you that we make tough choices to find readable and affordable texts.

A few years ago, my department switched from a very dense, theoretical textbook to one that is more "magazine" format (think lots of pictures, very short sections with headers). We had been with the former text for a decade. All faculty pored over fifteen texts in order to choose the new one, and we were very sensitive to content and price. What's funny is that, on the student evaluations, this new text wasn't rated any more positively than the more dense text. Unfortunately, students also didn't give comments so we could know what they didn't like.

Some end-of-term evaluations will ask open-ended questions about the textbook. Others will just have you "score" the textbook (1–5, or "Excellent" to "Poor," etc.) Whether or not your evals offer this opportunity, use the comments to let your professor know what you liked or didn't like about the text. I can't say that every faculty or department pays attention to this information, but many certainly do. If your class text needs to change due to content or price, your voice might very well be able to make that happen. Use it!

The Career Note

In thinking about being prepared for class, I thought about what preparedness looks like in the workplace. I asked a LinkedIn expert who blogs at *AvidCareerist.com* what happens if an employee fails to locate external resources when they are needed for a particular task:

> *This starts at the job interview, before students even land a job. Very few people research prospective employers before going to an interview.*

> *The downside to failing to prepare:*

> 1. *You don't have any questions to ask the employer during the interview.*

> 2. *You don't know if the company has a successful business model—or if they even have a business model.*

> 3. *You don't know if the company is growing. That's important because growth companies provide more opportunities for advancement than companies that are treading water or shrinking.*

> *The upside to preparing:*

> 1. *You ask intelligent questions during your interviews that make you stand out from other applicants.*

> 2. *You don't get your career stuck in a company that isn't going anywhere.*

> *Donna, LinkedIn/career coaching*

16. ■ Work Ethic

What You Might Think:

Work ethic? That doesn't matter as much in college because I'm not getting paid.

What Your Professor Thinks:

Your work ethic in college is your work ethic, despite the environment.

The Real Story

Some conversations with students will stick in my mind forever. A chat with Trent is one of them: Trent was my advisee and had taken multiple classes with me. He was fine producing mediocre work; I knew he was capable of so much more.

Trent always comprehended what we were doing in class at a high level. When we talked about using the assertive message in my Intro to Communication class, Trent said, "Wow, I used that last night with my brother, and I couldn't believe what a difference it made." Then he gave an effective example.

During my Interpersonal Communication class, where we discuss dynamics in family, professional, and romantic relationships, Trent joked about some of the concepts, but once class ended, he said that the class changed his life. He had a new girlfriend, and he was using the communication strategies almost daily to strengthen their relationship.

Although Trent knew the material, he did not apply what he knew to his assignments. Trent's work was often late, and when he submitted it, the quality was … well … not there.

One day, I decided to have a heart-to-heart with Trent. I said, "What's up? You clearly get this material, but I'm not seeing that in your work. I would love to be able to see you get the grades that you deserve, based on your knowledge. You know a lot about communication!"

Trent shocked me with his reply.

With a straight face but a relaxed smile, he said, "I just don't need to stress in school. I have never been a very good student anyway."

Confused, I said, "Well, isn't this the time to change that? What you did in high school doesn't matter now. College is the place to build your work ethic."

"I will," Trent said, "when I go to work."

"When you go to work?" I asked, quizzically.

"Yeah," Trent said. "When I get paid money, I know I'll do better."

There are many, many students who do not share Trent's perceptions about building a work ethic in college.

Take Allie. She was one of my highest-achieving students—a high school student taking college classes. Allie was going to graduate with her high school diploma and her first two years of college completed simultaneously. Not easy!

Allie was the opposite of Trent: she completed her work very early. She was constantly in my office checking on her grades and ensuring that she was on the right track. Allie also heavily involved herself in on-campus activities; she was a leader of several clubs and part of the Honor Society.

I remember talking to Allie about how she juggles it all. I knew that Allie's parents worked varied shifts and that sometimes she had to care for her siblings. Allie simply said, "I have to because this will be what changes my life."

Allie had a fire in her. Coasting was not in her vocabulary. She was hell-bent to build a work ethic that will likely be a part of her always.

The Backstory

I really believe that some students think that their work ethic will just "fall into place" once they are paid employees.

My take on that? (Because, of course, you want to know, right?)

Who you are in this moment is who you are!

If your work ethic is crap right now, then that *is* your work ethic!

Own it, be proud, or work to change it. But don't fool yourself into believing that you will miraculously behave differently once a job is in front of you.

Sure, we put on different faces with our friends and families. I don't deny that. But our motivation, effort, drive for excellence, reliability, and commitment to a task well done is pretty consistent. For some of you, college may be the first place where you need to be accountable for the quality of your work. And we could say that you are "paid" for that work in your grade.

I know it's hard to look at your grades this way sometimes. Grades don't feel tangible, but the workload leading up to them sure as hell does! The way you approach that workload says a *ton* about you:

Do you tackle your work head-on? Or do you slack and make excuses?

If it's the latter, then there is a good chance that the second you face a job you don't want to do at your real job, you may slack there as well. Will a paycheck really change poor work habits like procrastination, lack of attention to detail, unreliability, or an absence of motivation? Maybe, but it probably won't be immediate, and look at the benefits of good performance that you missed in college!

Ask Yourself This:

Do I believe that college doesn't really matter because my grades won't make a difference in what I eventually want to do with my life? What words would I use to describe my work ethic right now? Am I happy with what I think about my work ethic?

Think This:

The work I do in college can make a big difference for me when it comes time to find a job. It's not just about my grades but about my work style. If I'm someone who shows a lot of commitment and perseverance to hard work, I will be able to give examples of those situations when I'm interviewing for jobs. I will also have a better likelihood of impressing

my professors, which may mean they will support me with recommendation letters or referrals later.

Not That:

I'll figure out what type of work ethic I have when I need to worry about that. College is just for having fun. I don't have to get serious about work just yet.

Wrong. College is prime time to get serious about work—while you are also having some fun!

Say This:

May I submit work for early review?

Will you give me some help? I'm not sure I'm understanding the concepts.

I want to do well in this class and have a goal of getting a 3.5. Are there any recommendations you can make?

I am wondering if you can give me some feedback on this paper. I worked on it early so I could show it to you.

These are all phrases of someone with a high work ethic!

Not That:

I didn't get my paper done. May I turn it in late?

Why did you give me a C? I thought I did better than that.

I missed the last two weeks. Can I still pass this class?

Ugh. What you're telling me to do requires too much work. Can't we make this easier?

(Not surprisingly, all of these statements can threaten others' perception about your work ethic. There are professional ways to deal with these issues. You'll find tips in related chapters about late work and absences.)

The End Note

The only person who defines your work ethic is you.

Trent was really comfortable with where he was in his life. He enjoyed hanging out with his friends and having fun. He attended class regularly, but, other than his good attendance in class, working just above the bare minimum was satisfactory.

I know that Trent did actually get a job at a local fast-food restaurant while he was in college. By the time he finished his two-year degree, he moved into management there. Trent also landed a girlfriend. Things were looking very serious, like engagement serious. Suddenly, it seemed like Trent was no longer content with a work ethic that wasn't consistent with the new roles he was playing in his life. I know that he did a hard reexamine on himself, and he turned things around.

I have to give Trent credit. He was real with me—with himself.

Be honest with yourself about the habits you're creating.

These habits don't have to define you forever.

Without a doubt, and at any point, you have all the power to change what you're doing and the way you are doing it.

Best part? There are so, so many people in college—from your professors to all the support staff—who are there to support you.

The Career Note

I was eager to find out if employers believe that students' poor work ethic magically transforms once in the workplace. Here's what I found out:

> *In most organizations, professional employees are expected to manage multiple responsibilities in fast-paced environments. Competing priorities can change quickly based on business needs, so employers rely on team members who demonstrate strong work ethic through accountability and determination. Professionals in today's workforce must achieve results with minimal resources.*
>
> *In my experience, the foundational work ethic that a student develops in college is critical to their future success in the workplace. If a student is able to effectively "juggle" their academic work with other commitments such as employment and/or extra-curricular activities, it is a strong indicator that they have the skills to successfully handle numerous projects at work.*
>
> *Many employers believe that future behavior can be predicted from prior behavior, so it is important for students to develop a strong work ethic prior to graduation. Employers will look for proven examples*

of these experiences during the interview process, whether the behavior was in an academic environment or elsewhere.

Jonathan, retail industry

---

17. Doing Things Your Way

What You Might Think:

I read the instructions, and yeah, you've given me feedback on how I should go about this project. I have a different idea, and I'm going to go with that.

What Your Professor Thinks:

My suggestions are meant to help you improve your work and are based on what I know to be the standards and requirements. You can choose to do things your way, but your grade may suffer.

The Real Story

Monroe was a student with superstrong opinions. Typically, I appreciate this because working with different personality types is what makes classes so interesting and what helps me grow as an educator.

In Monroe's case, his strong opinions weren't just limited to class discussion; he wanted to change the parameters of every class assignment. Let me put this in some context: Monroe was already in a class with considerable flexibility. It was an advanced public speaking course, and many of the students were already industry professionals (Monroe wasn't yet working and was one of the younger students in the class). Since I knew that most of the students already gave presentations as part of their jobs, I gave all students the type of speech (training program, informative briefing, problem–solution report, etc.), but they could choose any topic that fit.

Monroe eagerly approached me with ideas for an informative topic: to inform his audience on why they should adopt a certain exercise program. Monroe didn't have any particular expertise on this subject; instead, he really wanted to persuade about exercise. The only problem was that the speech requirements were to teach the audience something new—to be informative rather than persuasive.

I went back and forth with Monroe, trying to come up with creative iterations of his idea since he was so passionate about it. At every turn, I asked him to consider his audience, that people generally have a lot of strong feelings about exercise, and that he really had to offer fresh information. When he sent me his outline, it was clear that Monroe was taking none of my advice. He essentially had a persuasive speech about exercise.

At a certain point, there was nothing further I could do. Monroe was set on that speech. When he delivered it, the audience was completely confused and, quite frankly, bored. The information was not new, and the structure was all over the place. Of course, Monroe disputed his low grade. I went back and showed him the assignment requirements and all of my subsequent e-mails with clear recommendations that he should change course.

I'm sure you wouldn't be surprised to hear that every subsequent speech of Monroe's went this exact same way.

The Backstory

Have you ever watched the show *The Next Food Network Star*? In short, three Food Network stars—big ones: Bobby Flay, Giada De Laurentiis, and Alton Brown—give contestants coaching and are brutally honest about what they need to do to win over Food Network executives and score their own show.

Most contestants take their mentor's advice to the best of their ability. However, some blatantly say, "I'm going to do things my own way." Case in point: one contestant was recommended to show more enthusiasm, to which that person responded, "I can't kick up my laid-back personality because it's just not who I am." Another contestant argued with their mentor that a "culinary point of view" isn't as important as being a strong presenter.

Are you reading this and thinking that these contestants are nuts? I mean, here's a competition with mentors who are successful television chefs. Mentors who have nothing to gain or lose by the contestants scoring a show or going home. Their feedback comes with goodwill, the sole desire to improve the performance of their mentees. Whether or not the mentees act on the advice is up to them. And in the case of the dissenting contestants? Let's just say you won't see either of them on the Food Network. They were both ultimately sent home.

This reality show totally correlates to student–professor dynamics, particularly when students either ask for feedback that they don't take or when the student interprets an assignment, project, etc., in some other way than it was intended.

As you know, I do review work ahead of time. My feedback is typically substantive and thoughtful. Most students take my suggestions and then improve their work. But other students, like Monroe, are determined to go their own way.

What then? I have to grade the work accordingly. If the work meets the objectives of the assignment, then the grade will reflect that the standards were met. If objectives were not met, then the grade will be low.

I wish the next events unfolded like they do on *The Next Food Network Star*: Giada, Alton, and Bobby usually receive humility from their contestants: "Yeah, I took a risk and it didn't really pan out."

But when you're a professor and students do their own thing on assignments, the negative outcome is because *we* graded unfairly or *we* didn't give good feedback.

What I ask you to remember is that professors are *just* like these superstar mentors (except work kitchens may or may not have a sink, and it's usually tiny). We have *nothing* to lose or gain by you taking our advice.

Think about it: your professors all have their degrees. Our education is over. When we give you feedback about your work, particularly in advance of grading your work, that advice is meant to make your work *better*. We want you to improve!

Ask Yourself This:

Before I decide to interpret an assignment different-ly, have I made sure I understand the instructions? Have I talked over my idea with my professor? If my professor felt I should do something different, what is my rationale for going with my original idea? Am

I afraid that I won't be an independent thinker or strong enough to do take a direction I feel is right?

Think This:

When my professor gives me feedback, I can choose to make changes or not. If I don't make changes, I need to accept the consequences if my work doesn't meet the assignment requirements. I can also have a discussion with my professor about how my idea can adapt to the assignment. If I can't end up doing what I wanted, that doesn't mean I can't think for myself. It means that I am getting advice on how to do the best work I can do.

Not That:

My professor doesn't like my idea because it isn't hers. She only wants us to do what she thinks is right. I am not in college to be brainwashed.

A student who wanted to go their own way once used that word: "brainwashed." It is true that classes are fraught with requirements, and you may feel like you can't be as free a thinker as you'd like. But remember that requirements are often meant for you to practice following a particular structure. You'll do a lot more writing, speaking, etc., and you'll be able to get as creative as you want when you have a basic framework that you've already learned.

Say This:

If you have been given feedback and you still want to go your own way, be honest about your strong feelings, and become informed about any ramifications. You do not want to be blindsided!

I see that you suggested I do the assignment this way. I really wanted to go about it like this (then explain). Can you tell me your concerns about my approach?

or

I respect what you're telling me, but I feel really strongly about moving forward in my direction. Can you tell me what consequences I might face? What might happen with my grade?

or

I see where you're coming from with your suggestions. How could I keep some of what I'm trying to do and adopt some of what you're saying as well?

Not That:

Crickets

… and then doing what you want without a discussion.

or

I'm doing what I want to do because I don't agree with the requirements.

You have every right to disagree with your professor's recommendations. Just have a transparent discussion about it first.

The End Note

If you've ever read or watched an interview with someone who is successful, you might have noticed that they often talk about how they charted their own course and did something totally different from the norm. I realize those messages can be incredibly confusing, particularly in college, when you might feel constrained and confined by requirements and standards to receive a grade.

Sometimes, your way needs to give way to those requirements. Other times, you may decide that you can stomach going your way and you are fine with the outcome.

Either way, keep open communication, then make a mindful decision.

I know you'll make one that is right for you.

The Career Note

I wondered what happens at work when a supervisor gives instructions and an employee "dumbs them down," so to speak. This might be due to low self-confidence in abilities, lack of desire to adhere to the standards, or inclination to change the project despite very clear parameters. I asked someone whose world is very technical and doesn't allow for many interpretations of "the rules."

> *The world of Cybersecurity is a professionally focused environment. When requested to complete a security project following outlined parameters, it's expected that I do my best to meet or exceed those standards. Information that affects people's lives is no trivial matter. Taking the easy road by oversimplifying or dumbing down the project immediately calls my abilities, skill, and knowledge into question.*

Additionally, that reflects on the entire department. It's gravely important to remember your project may represent more than just yourself. This will undoubtedly come up in future performance reviews or when being considered for a promotion. Instead, consider at least meeting or exceeding any standards set by instructions, even if you have to work harder.

Eric, cybersecurity/engineer

18. Asking for Help in Enough Time to Use It/ Avoiding a Zero

What You Might Say:

I didn't understand the assignment and didn't ask for help. I'll take a zero.

What Your Professor Thinks:

I wish I had known so I could have helped you. Any points are better than a zero!

The Real Story

In week eight of a ten-week term, Ty emailed me: "My average is a D. Can you tell me what's up?"

My response: "Looks like you missed the annotated bibliography. That was worth 50 points. Also, several discussion questions weren't completed."

From Ty: "I didn't know how to do the bibliography, so I took a zero on that. And the discussion questions. I didn't know what you were asking."

Then there was Breanna, who submitted an early paper. Her proactiveness was awesome, but the paper was fraught with organizational issues. I made suggestions, but Breanna didn't revise, despite having another week before the due date. When I asked why, she said, "I still didn't know what to do!"

And Avery: Avery e-mailed two hours before an assignment deadline: "Can you explain the citation requirements?"

Citations take one, if not two, full class sessions to explain. Even if I gave Avery a quick citation lesson, she was too close to the deadline to apply the information.

What is the result of missed opportunities for help? Ty didn't learn how to do a bibliography, nor did he gain the experience of receiving clarification on an assignment. Likewise for Avery and those citations. Breanna missed the chance to practice using feedback for revision.

I could give you innumerable examples of learning issues caused by not seeking assistance or doing so without time to use it. And along with those learning issues inevitably came low grades, or worse, zeroes.

The Backstory

I am passionate about every topic in this book, but the help issue—in all its varieties—is a problem that seemingly has no end.

Remember, as a college student, your job is to learn and, sometimes, to need help with your learning. It is your professor's job to teach you and provide that help.

The caveat is that your professor won't beg you to get help. The onus is always on you to ask for it!

Be selfish about your learning and the "process" of learning. Believe that you deserve to connect with and comprehend the vast information you're being taught in all of your college classes. When you can't figure out what you need to know/do, then it's time to request help!

But here's the magic: request the assistance in a time frame that allows you to take the next step in your learning (in other words, what you need to do for the reading, assignment, exam, etc.). Otherwise, you are shortchanging your learning process *and* waving a huge procrastination flag to your professor. In the workplace, being seen as someone who waits until the last minute to find answers or complete work can destroy your reputation, plain and simple.

Remember, you don't always need to be confused to ask for help. Maybe you've worked early and you want to ensure you're on the right track. Some professors will prereview your work. Others won't because they don't want to go through the exercise of grading twice (even if they aren't giving you a grade with the early review, it still takes time). For professors who willingly provide help, they anticipate you'll use the feedback.

Many students who submit an assignment for early review mistakenly assume their first pass is good to go. This is counterintuitive to learning in college—and in life, really. Learning is meant to be a layered process: you are taught an idea/concept—whatever—and that information builds on further knowledge and, ultimately, application (think assignments, tests, etc.). After application, revision typically follows.

When your professor advises how to improve an upcoming assignment, that aspect of your learning offers more than a grade. You have the opportunity to show that you can accept feedback and act on it. So again, when help is given, leave yourself enough time to implement it.

If you don't ask for help at all, that's obviously a bigger issue—one that could cost you a low grade or a zero. Taking a zero is never a good idea. You want any points you can get! Think about it: a missed assignment that earns zero points puts pressure on the remaining assignments. Then you need to earn high points to average up the zeroes—depending on what you're trying to earn in the class, of course.

Ask for help early, and keep asking until you get what you need. If you must, do part of the assignment and receive *some* points. Better than no points at all!

If you miss the assignment and receive a zero but your professor accepts late work at a 50 percent penalty, take that 50 percent—or whatever you can get!

Let's look at a breakdown of this in plain math with Lane and Shalonda:

Lane		Shalonda	
Assignment 1	40/50	Assignment 1	50/50
Assignment 2	40/50	Assignment 2	40/50
Assignment 3	37/50	Assignment 2	45/50
Exam 1	80/100	Exam 1	90/100
Assignment 4	0 not submitted	Assignment 4	30/50 late penalty
Assignment 5	42/50	Assignment 5	50/50

Exam 2	79/100	Exam 2	85/100
TOTAL	318/450 = 71%	TOTAL	390/450 = 87%
Had Lane taken the 50% penalty on assignment 4	348/450 = 77%	Had Shalonda taken a zero rather than partial credit	360/450 = 80%

Those few points make a difference, don't they? And this example just shows *one* missing/late assignment. You and I both know that one missed/late assignment easily leads to another.

I can't leave this topic without reminding you that sometimes your zero may be because your professor didn't log the grade or receive your assignment. Professors make mistakes: we transpose numbers, etc. So always, *always* stay on top of your grades.

In closing, let me just sneak in one more reminder: avoid a zero altogether! Get that help in a timely manner! Remember that the overall goal is for you to learn new things, to demonstrate your knowledge In assignments, projects, tests, etc., and to receive a grade that "measures" your ability to do both!

Ask Yourself This:

What do I believe that asking for help says about me? That I'm lazy? Stupid? A failure? What negative consequences have I faced because I waited too long to ask for help? Have I ever had a positive experience receiving help and putting it into place? Did I feel proud? Smart?

Think This:

I'm putting myself and my professor at a big disadvantage when I either don't ask for help at all or I ask for help too close to when my assignment is due.

You deserve time to put the help you're given into action. Your prof deserves the opportunity to straighten out your confusion.

Not That:

I don't really need any help. I'll figure this out on my own.

This only works if it's true.

The prof is obligated to help me whenever.

The prof is well within her rights to say that your request is too close to the deadline and that the feedback is too much for you to implement now.

Say This:

First, see when your assignment is due. Then, try to do something, *anything,* to help yourself. Then you'll be able to tell your professor you tried:

I read Chapter 6, and I got stuck on page 49.

or

I think I have an idea of what we're supposed to be doing, but I want to make sure I'm correct.

or

I read the assignment and here's what I think, but I think it might be incorrect.

Not That:

Saying nothing at all is the worst thing you can do. Other statements to avoid:

You didn't help me, and that's why I didn't do well.

Blame isn't going to get you anywhere. If you aren't getting what you need, go to those office hours (again!), send another e-mail—whatever. If you still don't understand, reiterate the areas you do understand and ask the professor to explain the information in a different way:

I get what I'm supposed to be doing up through step five, but I'm completely confused after that point. I'm sorry to make you cover this again, but I want to make sure I get it.

I didn't feel like I should ask for help.

Unless you are making the request right before the deadline, you should always ask.

The End Note

I want to end on a high note. There *are* students who take immediate action to get what they need and they learn a great deal in the process:

Meghan struggled with writing and needed lots of time to get help and implement recommendations. Sometimes, Meghan requested a second review on her work. You can imagine how early she had to start writing to make this happen. Meghan learned a heck of a lot about her own strengths and challenges. The habits she cultivated in college will easily transfer into writing that she may need to edit in the workplace.

Jamie, a solid writer and public speaker, sent in his rough outline three weeks early. Good thing. His topic was a confusing angle on the Federal Reserve. The topic was way over my head, but not so for my political science colleague. Since Jamie worked early, we tag-teamed, and Jamie found a logical approach. Jamie gained new insights on crafting a strong topic and making that topic comprehensible for an audience.

Jeneen and Benjamin took my class as a couple. They were fiercely proactive about clarifying instructions for every assignment. Brian actually came to my office with prewritten questions! Clearly, they knew how to get their academic needs met.

Sure, these students received high grades. No surprise, right? But more importantly, they displayed courage: they knew they didn't need to have all the answers, but they were brave enough to ask questions and seek resources.

Keep in mind that your professor is not your only resource. You have librarians and academic support centers (think library, tutoring, etc.) available, too. Find out all the places that you can get help and then, by all means, grab that help that you need!

The Career Note

How does asking for help prepare you for the workplace? I asked an executive who leads major nonprofits in fundraising efforts:

> *You are faced with a daunting project. Maybe it is to launch a new business concept or to propose a change amongst your development team. Maybe you're trying to obtain fresh leads for your next writing project. When we are faced with big projects, the best way to proceed is to engage others in our quest. Asking for help is a natural step in building the best "product." Asking for advice, insight and overall input from a trusted advisor/instructor/mentor will enable that person to give you the information that you are seeking and maybe a bit of unexpected assistance, too. By seeking another person's counsel, you are opening yourself up to aspects that you might not have thought of on your own.*
>
> *When asking for help, be considerate of that person's available time and your pressing deadlines—planning ahead will go a long way to your benefit if you demonstrate your thoughtfulness. When you receive "help" from others, show gratitude. Thank them for their assistance—a simple e-mail or quick note card will do. Asking for help is a skill that you will use in your professional and personal life. We are not alone in this big world.*
>
> *Sharon, nonprofit executive*

19. ■ Late Work

The Backstory

What You Might Say:

May I turn in this assignment late?

or

May I have an extension?

What Your Professor Thinks:

I'd have to give that option to twenty-eight other people in the class.

The Real Story

Tanner says after class, "I was really confused over the transitions, so I didn't turn in the outline."

Lladro sends an e-mail: "My computer totally crashed. Can I have a three-day extension?"

Henry stopped in my office: "My grandpa got sick, and I had to go out of town. I thought I'd have enough time."

This is just a small sampling of late-work issues. These students may not realize that one late assignment (if allowed) can risk more, not to mention less time to work on subsequent assignments. A slippery slope!

The Backstory

I've agonized over late work for many years. Do I allow one student to submit late because of an emergency? Or, like many colleagues, do I have a zero-tolerance policy? I'll tell you where I've landed before this chapter ends.

First, why does late work happen? The main culprits: procrastination, life emergencies, and failing to ask for help in enough time. In my opinion, urgency over late work has diminished. No more excuses. Some students casually shrug and say, "I just didn't get to it." An extension is expected, and without penalty, which perpetuates a lousy work ethic.

Speaking of work ethic, I realized a year ago that I was doing no good for my students by accepting late work. I wasn't emphasizing the gravity of deadlines or the consequences of missing them. For example, I wrote for *USA Today* various times. The deadline was 9:00 a.m. Submit late, and they'd never ask again. Same deal with my promotion-package deadline: March 11. Submit March 12, and no promotion. Done and done.

Flexible deadlines hurt me as well. My inbox compiled late assignments that slipped to the bottom of the grade pile—and often to the term's end. I couldn't grade late work before other students' on-time work, could I? No!

I recognize the difference between habitual lateness and a onetime emergency. An emergency does *not* consist of a student e-mailing me an hour before a deadline and needing help. Hello! Procrastination, anyone?

I concluded that my only choice was a zero-tolerance policy. I needed to send a clear message that students should adjust their schedules according to the deadline.

A lot of professors don't accept late work. Be prepared for that. But more than anything, care about how late work affects *you*. Not so much the grade, but your stress level associated with late work.

Most college work "scaffolds"; if you don't know what's going on with one assignment, you'll likely have to revisit that information again. Save yourself from confusion a second, third, or fourth time! Get help! Feedback also scaffolds: your professor expects you to apply suggestions to future work.

As mentioned, late assignments threatens future assignments. Are you prepared to double your workload to catch up? What if you forget critical information and, when you get back to the late assignment, it's harder than ever? See how much pressure this adds to your life?

Your professor's time isn't necessarily your problem, but let me share some insight here: most professors have multiple classes submitting work at the same time. We may grade for hours each day or many hours over multiple days. I can't stand assignments piling up, so I finish within twenty-four to forty-eight hours. You may think, "But some professors don't return work until weeks after I've submitted it." I'll address that when talking about your rights in Chapter 29.

Back to the issue: your professor grades multiple assignments, then finishes and preps for upcoming curriculum. If three students (that's a conservative number!) submit late work—all

on different days—your professor has to stop prepping or helping other students who weren't late. All you may get is a letter
or number and no feedback. That hurts you and your potential
for future success in the class.

One last issue with late work: Have you ever tried to frantically
finish work in a different class or skip a class to get more time?
Doing work in an unrelated class is a dangerous practice. First
of all, your professor could find out, and then if you struggle
there, you'll have no leg to stand on because you weren't
paying attention. Second, it's hard to multitask when you're
distracted by class happenings.

If you skip a class to catch up in another one (or that one),
you'll have to weigh how much time you're really gaining and
if you will actually work. If you check social media, you'll waste
the time with no benefit. Then you risk falling behind in the
missed class. Not worth it!

Ask Yourself This:

> *Why don't I get work done on time? What negative
> consequences have I faced because of late work?
> What am I willing to change so I can keep this from
> happening?*

Think This:

> *If I plan in advance, I can get help with my work and
> have time to do it. I will feel proud for working early
> and more relaxed about asking questions, and I'll
> probably be happier with my grade outcome.*

Not That:

> *One late penalty won't hurt.*

It might. And what if your professor has a zero-tolerance policy? Then you will have a zero!

or

> *I'll have time to finish other assignments, even if this one is late.*

There is just no way to know how long future work will take you.

or

> *I'll get to this before the end of the term.*

Think about how bogged down you will be with *other* things by then.

Say This:

After you've reviewed the syllabus to see if your professor has a late policy, say:

> Professor, my assignment is going to be late. I won't make this a habit. I reviewed the late policy, and I see that I can turn in the assignment with a 50 percent penalty. I will have the assignment to you in forty-eight hours. Would that be all right?

You may relinquish any rights to ask for help, but you can add:

> Would you answer questions if I have them?

Important: submit the late work at the agreed-upon time! Find out if there is a variation in penalty:

Professor, what is the latest date you'd be willing to accept this assignment? What penalty am I facing if I turn it in in two weeks rather than one?

If your professor has no late policy, you can try:

Professor, I realize you don't accept late work. I won't give excuses to make you change your mind. If I were to turn it in, could I receive any credit?

If you were confused about the assignment, say:

Professor, I needed help and I didn't turn in my assignment. I want to be successful next time. Can you get me on track? I will be sure to ask for help much sooner.

The professor may agree to get you up to speed but still not let you submit the work.

If you are usually on time and facing a life situation, say,

Professor, I am usually on time and even early with my assignments. A situation happened that is out of my control. I'm at risk of turning in my assignment late. I took a look at the syllabus and reviewed the late policy. I hope I don't need it, but I wanted to be prepared. I would be glad to show you the progress I've already made.

Your professor will appreciate you being proactive and taking responsibility.

Never, ever demand that your professor grade your work within a certain time frame. It is not fair to the students who met the deadline. Your professor will get to your work when she can.

Not That:

May I please have an extension for this assignment?

Your professor has to offer this to everyone if he offers it to you.

or

I had a really bad thing happen, and I couldn't get my assignment done. I really need to turn it in late!

No excuses! Solve the problem instead. Your professor wants to know what you intend to do about your late work.

or

It's not fair that you don't accept late work!

Life emergencies happen, but your professor expects you to schedule yourself in a way that reduces the risk of life events hindering your deadlines. When you wait 'til the last minute to even start your work, you risk more unexpected situations getting in the way.

The End Note

The first term of my zero-tolerance late-work policy produced some of the harshest student evaluations of my career. Students liked me, but suddenly I was seen as very strict. I transparently explained why I don't accept late work and how it can significantly harm a professional persona. My explanation didn't matter when a student descended upon my office one day in tears.

"This is so unfair!" Samai said. "I played baseball with a friend, fell asleep, got into an argument with my mom, and then realized that my assignment was due."

(This student habitually e-mailed an hour prior to deadlines with last-minute questions.)

"The zero is recoverable. It's early in the term," I told Samai. "Let's talk about the bigger problem of procrastination and figure that out."

Samai couldn't get past the zero grade to consider the overall habit. Take a hard look at how you prioritize school work. Every class requires time—and even more time if that subject is difficult for you. Are you prepared to cultivate this work ethic now to schedule the time you need and still meet your deadlines? Or would you rather stress and scramble, likely not doing work of strong quality and risking your professional reputation? Is that who you want to be?

Only you know the answer. The beauty of college is that you can change these behaviors and create different habits before the negative patterns hold you back.

The Career Note

One of employers' biggest complaints about college graduates is lack of work ethic, specifically punctuality and ability to meet deadlines (studies reported in 2013–2014 on CNBC and in *Time* magazine[1]). I wanted an industry perspective on

---

[1] http://www.cnbc.com/2014/01/29/the-surprising-reason-college-grads-cant-get-a-job.html

http://business.time.com/2013/11/10/the-real-reason-new-college-grads-cant-get-hired/#ixzz2rlEKc6zk colleagues who can't meet deadlines. What impact does this have on the team and the workplace at large? What is the best advice for students who struggle to meet deadlines?

> *I work in the legal field, and deadlines are a very serious matter. Some deadlines are set by statute and cannot be missed or the client's case is negatively and irrevocably impacted. This can result in bar complaints and malpractice lawsuits. Attorneys who constantly miss deadlines are not respected by other attorneys or the judicial officers they appear before. Even arriving late for court will cause some judges to sanction you. If documents are submitted late, often the court cannot consider them and is not required to give a continuance. You rarely see experienced attorneys missing any deadlines. Law school is where lawyers learn to meet these critical deadlines—the students are given too much work to possibly get done, short deadlines, and are essentially required to participate in various extracurricular activities in order to find employment after law school. What they are learning is to focus, determine what needs to be done by when, and then make it happen. It's very important for students to practice this level of timeliness and the time management and organization that results in timeliness while still in school. Once they graduate and get jobs, there are no second chances.*
>
> *Susan, law*

20. Leaving Early/ Arriving Late

What You Might Say:

May I leave early today? I have an appointment.

What Your Professor Thinks:

What do I do about the other thirty-two students who want to leave early?

The Real Story

Barrie came up to me on a break and said, "I have a terrible headache and feel like I'm going to throw up. Can I go home?"

Earlier that day, Dionne e-mailed saying that she has to work an hour later than usual and will need to be late to class.

Simon catches me before class starts and says, "My girlfriend needs a ride home from work, and I need to leave early."

Most students don't realize that professors have already heard all 1,872+ reasons why students can't come on time or need to leave before class ends.

The Backstory

I understand that there are times when students legitimately need to cut class short or when they can't make it on time. Unexpected things happen: traffic, life situations, etc. I also appreciate students' courtesy in telling me that they need to depart class before it ends. But here's the truth: students choose class times, just like I choose those times to teach.

I have to arrange my life to be in class based on my teaching schedule. I anticipate that students will arrange their lives to be in class at the times they've chosen. I also expect them to stay for the *entire* class—or at least for 99 percent of the term.

If a student needs to leave for an appointment, to catch a plane—whatever—unless those situations are absolutely necessary (e.g., an appointment for an emergent doctor's visit; attending a family member's funeral), then I question if they think that class times are flexible enough to schedule right over them. (Psst: they're not!)

If you have a trip or special appointment preplanned (like before school starts), tell your professor on the first day or the second you know about it. If you start a new job, you'd negotiate this time *before you start*: "Listen, I hate to ask for time off so early, but my family has a trip planned. Can we work this out?" Hopefully, you can work it out. The same courtesy applies to your professor.

Sometimes, students ask to leave early in order to study for another class. Your professor thinks, *So, my class is less important?* or *You put off studying for that other class, and now you're willing to sacrifice my class?* Not a good message to send.

Quite often, the student's job gets in the way, such as by a shift change, new start time, etc. This is understandable, and your professor would empathize with the fact that not every supervisor will care about your school schedule. We know many students juggle one job or more to stay in school. However, I have had countless students ask if they can come in a half hour or even an hour late (or leave early) to accommodate their known work schedule. How is this reasonable for the student, the professor, or other students in the class?

Your professors need to know that you perceive your education as a job, too. You won't lose money when you are late or miss a class, but you lose "pay" in other ways: points, details on assignments/tests, and a challenged relationship with your professor.

Before I move on, here's one other reason students ask to leave early (or come in late): scheduling two classes that overlap. I have taught at 5:15 p.m., and students will ask if they can arrive fifteen minutes late because their previous class doesn't end until 5:30 p.m. These students try to strike the same "leave early" deal on the other side. A professor can't allow this—even though, really, the college should look at how class times are starting and ending so students aren't in this predicament.

Remember, regardless of the reason you can't be in the full class, your professor can never say, "Yes, that's fine," without giving that option (or potentially ticking off) other students in the class.

In fact, my standard response goes like this:

> I understand that you may need to leave early. I cannot give you permission to do so without upsetting others in class. This is college. You do not need

my permission to leave early. It is your choice to leave early, so do what you need to do.

Then the inevitable question: "But will I lose points?"

Here things get sticky. I have had students sit in class for ten minutes then leave, expecting to receive credit for the full day. Similarly, some students walk into class fifteen minutes before class ends, thinking, *Hey, I showed my face for a few minutes. At least I was here!*

Some professors take attendance, and others don't. If they do, attendance patterns differ. There are professors who check at the beginning and end of class; there are professors who call roll once and that's it. Find out if attendance points are bundled with participation points. Know that even if they aren't, professors typically remember if you repeatedly missed parts of class. They may consider this when calculating your overall grade.

Ask Yourself This:

Do I frequently leave classes early or ask to leave early? Did I have a legitimate reason, or did I just not want to stay in class? What consequences have I faced due to leaving early (or showing up late)? What scheduling changes can I make to remain in class for the entire time?

Think This:

I can leave early once or twice in a quarter for a valid reason, and it probably won't have much effect on my standing in the class. However, my professor cannot give me permission to leave. I will take responsibility for any penalties I face for leaving

early. Most of all, I will take a hard look at my sched-
ule and make sure that I have enough time to be in
class and get to my other obligations on time.

Not That:

The prof won't notice if I leave early.

That may be true, but there is a greater likelihood that the professor *will* know. Even if he/she doesn't know your name, they will see you walk out the door.

It's my class time, and if I don't want to stay for the whole thing, that's my business. I'm paying for this.

Very true. Class time is yours. But you *are* paying for it. Don't you want to experience the benefit for your money (or financial aid)? Even if the class totally sucks, you still need the information that you'll receive during class in order to do your work and get your grade.

I have a good reason for leaving early.

As I've said before in these chapters, the "why" doesn't matter. Not because your professor doesn't care but because there's a job to be done, and you both signed on to complete it.

Say This:

Ideally, as soon as you know you need to leave early, say:

Dr. Jones, a situation has come up, and I need to leave class early today. I know this is not ideal. I do not plan to make this a regular habit (*if you are further along in the term, you can say:* As you know, I don't make it a habit of leaving early.)

I understand that I may face a penalty for this, and I am willing to be responsible for any work that I missed.

or

Professor, I'm going to be late on Thursday. It is unavoidable, and I will keep my overall lateness to a minimum *(or you can say that you haven't been late for class yet)*. I've reviewed the schedule. I see that Chapter 5 is going to be covered that day. I'll be sure to start on Chapter 5 and catch myself up to where the class is when I arrive.

Not That:

May I leave early because _____?

or

I shouldn't lose attendance points because I came in late/left early. That's not fair!

Every individual professor has the right to impose reasonable attendance policies. If your class involves a lot of group or paired work, your professor needs to have students there in order for those activities to go smoothly or actually happen at all. Therefore, if your professor has a stiff attendance policy that includes late arrival/early departure penalties, there is likely a good reason. The policy only stands to help your potential success in the class.

The End Note

With late arrivals and early departures, what we're really talking about is the general debate over attendance policies in college. Some people think college should not include attendance taking—that students who show up will naturally do better than those who don't, and the decision is individual. Others think it's necessary practice to keep students accountable and to ensure the possibility for community building in the classroom. Regardless, get familiar with the attendance/participation policy for your class (it's in the syllabus). Determine where leaving early and coming in late relates to that policy. If you are unsure, ask your professor for clarification.

Most of all, handle your early/late situation professionally and proactively. Avoid asking for special treatment. You will maintain a better working relationship with your professor. You may even receive more leniency. You may not, but at least you will know you approached the situation like a professional.

The Career Note

Many companies offer flexible start times, although some "hard" start times are required for meetings, etc. I asked a business consultant with a highly cited blog, *Workplacewisdom. com*, why students should establish positive time habits in college. How could frequent lateness later become an issue in the workplace?

> *In the workplace, a common assumption is that people who show up late don't really care and can't be counted on. Rushing into a meeting just as or after it starts makes you look like you can't get your act together. Tardiness carries its own natural consequences: You lose out on anything that*

occurs on a first-come, first-served basis, from parking spots to new equipment to special assignments. You may also miss your chance to participate in spot bonuses and promotion opportunities even if your work is otherwise perfectly good.

So practice being on time in school. Analyze your situation first: do you use an alarm or other trigger to tell you when it's time to get going? Do you respond to it immediately? Do you accurately calculate transfer time between locations? Do you squeeze in just one more thing before you head out, without noticing how quickly time is passing? Do you enjoy the adrenaline surge that comes with the last-minute risk?

Get over yourself. Experiment with your process and try being early. See how it feels not to be in a crazy rush and to start activities calmly, with full focus. Much more successful!

Liz, business consultant

21. After Absences: Dealing with What You Missed/Missing "Important" Work

What You Might Say:

I was out last Thursday. Can you tell me everything I missed? Did I miss anything important?

What Your Professor Thinks:

I don't prepare unimportant material. Should I hold a private class and cover fifty minutes of that material again?

The Real Story

Michael sent an e-mail: "I think I have the flu. Can you send me what I missed from class today?"

My response: "Michael, so sorry that you're sick. Review the class schedule. See what chapters we're working on. If you have questions after that, I'll answer them for you."

Then Michael: "But can't you just send me what I need? It would just be easier."

I reiterated my suggestion, and Michael found what he was looking for.

Eve missed a week of class. She asked, "Could you go over what I missed last Tuesday and Thursday?"

I said, somewhat jokingly, "You want me to repeat class all over again?"

Eve laughed, "No, of course not. I need to know if I missed anything important."

I repeated what I said to Michael.

"Oh, okay," Eve said, as if she never thought of doing this.

Some students do take responsibility for absences. Take Rahim: Rahim had an unexpected opportunity to travel with his family. Rahim said, "Mrs. Bremen, I'm going to miss two classes, and we're allowed two absences in the class. I looked at the schedule and printed out the assignments from the chapters you're covering. I don't see that I will fall behind. I can even have a draft of my outline to you before I go."

Wow. Nice way to take ownership of the absence, Rahim!

Before I close this section, you may be wondering how I addressed Eve's question about missing anything important. Let's put it this way: I'm rarely at a loss for words, but when this question arises, I am always a little stumped.

The Backstory

I wish I had a dollar for every time I'm asked to recap material due to student absences. This would be like asking a religious leader to repeat his sermon for you in your living room or asking your boss to call everyone back for a repeat meeting that you couldn't attend. Sound crazy? Of course it is!

I know that students innocently make this request, recalling their elementary or secondary years when someone could collect missed work for you. College just doesn't work this way. If you missed class, you bring yourself back up to speed.

Your first step is to look at the class schedule and see what happened while you were gone. I'm shocked by how few students do this. If the schedule says that the professor went over Chapter 6, then review Chapter 6. Your professor may post lecture notes, PowerPoint files, etc., in a course management system. Then you have what you need to catch *yourself* back up. Always look for the material before talking to the professor.

Next, ask a classmate or two if they can share notes from the day's events. Notice I said the "day's" events. If you missed more than a day or two, schedule an appointment with your professor to gauge your status in the class.

After you find out what occurred while you were gone, then—and only then—contact your professor. You can e-mail or visit during office hours, preferably before your next scheduled class. Translation: do not pop into the professor's office right before class is about to begin or launch into discussion just minutes before the class is going to start. Your professor won't be able to thoughtfully solve this problem when she is getting ready to teach.

With respect to the "Did I miss anything important today?" question, I have to be honest: it's probably one of the most insulting questions professors are asked, and I know students don't mean it to come out that way.

Students probably think, *Hey, it's good that I care about missing something really big, right?* They seek validation that missing class was "okay" (translation: justified) because nothing particularly noteworthy occurred (i.e., we didn't review for a test). Most students would consider *that* important information.

The truth is that the majority of professors work hard to plan a meaningful class session for you. Even if your professor has twenty years of experience and recycles lessons each term, that person still has to glance over what they will talk about. Granted, that's not a ton of prep, but it is prep nonetheless.

Other professors perpetually work to earn students' attention. They may create simple or elaborate PowerPoint presentations, locate YouTube videos or other multimedia, or pore over instructor's manuals to find just the right classroom activity to drive a point home. This effort may be for just one lesson! Prep also occurs on the professor's own time. Colleges don't provide dedicated prep time like elementary and secondary schools; the professor builds curriculum planning into his/her schedule, along with committee meetings, service to the institution and community, possibly research, meeting with students, etc. So, of course, your professor perceives the time they spent on your class *extremely* important.

Your course schedule may not reflect a "big" day either. Your professor may be returning papers, going over the results of a test, debriefing areas for help, etc. Your professor will perceive these days as critical; you may not. But what if there's a pop quiz? Pretty important, right?

Believe it or not, even if you miss a low-key day where the class is chatting it up, these days build community. That is very important!

Think about it this way: not every class is going to be riveting. Not every class session will feel important to you. There may be some days when you feel so bored that you want to pull your arm hairs one by one just to stay awake. The time and the fact that you were there still means something. You never know what important moment of learning will unexpectedly arise. View each class as its own meaningful experience.

Ask Yourself This:

What do I typically do about missed work? Do I take responsibility to catch myself up or expect the teacher to do it for me? How does falling behind make me feel? What consequences will I suffer? How would it feel to take responsibility for absences? Confident? Responsible?

and

Have I accepted that college classes typically contain information that is important for my learning, even if I don't see it that way at the time?

Think This:

Any time I miss class, it is always up to me to find out what I missed. I can ask my professor for help after I've taken action to help myself.

and

I should make every effort to attend as many classes as possible. Even if I find myself bored, I will try to find something valuable.

(Even if the only valuable aspect was that you actually showed up!)

Not That:

It's not my fault I missed class, and it's the professor's job to catch me up. That's what I'm paying for.

It is a professor's job to *teach* class, not to *reteach* class.

or

The professor will probably go over everything again so I can just catch up at the next class.

The greater likelihood is that the class moved on. If you raise your hand in class and say:

I missed class, so can you go over that again?

your classmates will probably roll their eyes and groan. They already sat through it.

or

It really won't make much of a difference if I miss this day. We probably aren't doing anything that important.

You just never know.

Say This:

Professor, I missed your class on Wednesday. I looked at the schedule and noticed that you covered Chapter 6 that day. I reviewed the material myself and asked Joann, who sits next to me, for the notes. I am a bit confused on *(insert specific question here)* and would like to ask some questions.

or

Professor, I missed your class on Wednesday. I looked at the schedule and noticed that you covered Chapter 6 that day. I have read Chapter 6 and also received information about the assignment from Joann, who sits next to me. I think I'm in good shape with catching up, but I just want to make sure I haven't missed anything.

If you absolutely must gauge whether one day is more "important" than another to miss, say:

Professor, I have to miss next Thursday, and I apologize for that. I try to keep my absences to a minimum *(only say this if it's true)*. I looked at the schedule, and I see that you're covering Chapter 11. We're taking our quiz a few days later, and I'll stay on track. I'd be glad to do the research on my own or ask a classmate to help me with notes.

Not That:

(Obviously ...)

Did I miss anything important?

I hope you'll permanently remove this from your question inventory.

or

Can you tell me what I missed?

or

Can you go over what I missed?

or

What should I do now?

What should you do now? Get on top of the schedule and material you missed. The materials are all likely right at your disposal, either via your schedule, another classmate, or other online course support.

The End Note

Some campuses have a student advocacy department to help you determine if you should stay with a class after you've missed a lot of it due to medical issues, a death in the immediate family, if you get called up from a reserve military unit for duty, etc. A neutral third party can help you figure out how to move forward. If your campus doesn't have a dedicated student advocacy department, counseling services, ACCESS/ Disability Services, or even an advisor (who isn't your professor) can help you figure out if you should take an incomplete or try to arrange another option.

Otherwise, remember what I said about your work ethic in college being a sign of your overall work ethic? A large part of work ethic is simply showing up and being present—regardless of if something "important" will happen.

If you haven't shown up, then remember that you have a better chance of working out your situation if you propose what you intend to do to catch up and show that you've taken all the ramifications into consideration. This is also a sign of a strong work ethic.

Be proactive and responsible rather than asking your professor to be reactive. More than that, attend class as much as you possibly can. And feel important for doing so.

The Career Note

In the workplace, I wondered, whose responsibility it is to get back up to speed when an employee misses work? How would an employee be perceived if they asked if anything "important" happened while they were out?

> *In healthcare, you are responsible for finding the information yourself, and you should also be provided key information upon your arrival. In my field of work, we give each other "reports" on our patients as we hand off our assignments to one another. It is important that the person going off shift provides important information to the person coming on shift.*
>
> *That being said, it is the employee's responsibility to check the patient's chart for their history; confirm orders, treatments, and information; and to check for any other important information that may exist. If the coworker who has given you the report accidentally forgets to give you a key piece of information, you need to be sure that you have found it. Missing something can cause harm to your patient; therefore, you are held liable if you perform an incorrect treatment, therapy, or dosage.*
>
> *Kelsi, healthcare*

Dealing with Technology

22.

Distracting Tech in Class: Texting/ Laptops/ Devices

What You Might Do:

Put your phone/device/laptop front and center on your desk, text during class, surf social media or unrelated-to-class websites.

What Your Professor Thinks:

Please don't distract those around you with your technology. I will have to call you out on it, privately or publicly, If It continues.

The Real Story

Delia and Greta sat next to each other but never exchanged words. In our lesson on listening, Greta piped up, "Some people can't listen because they're always texting." She looked right at Delia.

Yep. Delia was a texter—hiding her phone under her desk, tapping away every chance she got. She sat in front, so how could I miss her? Even more interesting, Delia never seemed oblivious to classroom happenings.

You can imagine Delia's mortification at being called out by Greta. "I don't think this is any of your business," she retorted.

Greta flared, "It is my business because it's very disrespectful to the professor, and it's very distracting to me."

Delia looked furious. A few other students looked guilty (they were texting, too). The room grew uncomfortably quiet. I told the women that we would discuss the matter privately. I knew the class was looking to me to call Delia out as well, but I didn't.

Here's another tech catastrophe: one of my colleagues asked, "Hey, is Phil Brown taking your class? I had him as a student, too. He has you in the evening, right? Just a warning: he's posting on Facebook throughout your class."

Hmm. In that situation, Phil wasn't distracting anyone else, but he was clearly distracted!

Then there was Jolina, my student who sat in the front row and read on her Kindle during every class session. Talk about putting in seat time. She didn't know what was happening in class. I wasn't quite sure why she was there.

The Backstory

My earlier teaching days used to involve students whispering or passing notes. Now, distraction is totally high-tech. Many professors ban technology from class. If they see you using tech at all, you'll have points deducted from your total grade. Other professors are more relaxed: bring on the phones, laptops—whatever—as long as it doesn't distract you or your classmates. And some professors embrace all the technology, using phones as student-response systems (think survey or multiple-choice questions on a board, and your smartphone helps you respond) or doing real-time tweet chats. If your professor's position on technology use isn't clear, always ask.

You may have to impose your own tech policies, which requires control. View these behaviors as a component of your overall work ethic. I'll explain.

Let's start with texting: texting during class is a bad idea any way you slice it. Aside from potentially distracting yourself and those around you, you're missing the class experience and, potentially, something important. It's tempting to respond quickly to that one message, but one message usually leads to many. Can you really send a single text and ignore the rest? Probably not!

Aside from texting, there is the "ever-present" phone (i.e., phones front and center on desks), begging for distraction. Students play games, respond to e-mails, or do all the things we do on our phones. Or, when they participate in group discussion, the second the conversation stops, out comes the phone.

I get it. Our phones are part of us. We love them. We need them. But how do you feel when you are with someone buried in their phone? Their behavior sends its own message. When I see a phone in a student's hand or on their desk, I perceive that they are just waiting, hoping for a distraction, not interested or invested in the class.

I realize that society has a phone obsession. However, any device that can take your attention at any second—this makes a statement about you. Do you want to be a distracted person, or a person who is truly present? Decide what message you want your phone to tell others about the professional you strive to be.

Another thing to consider about texting: when it distracts others, à la Greta and Delia. At the time, I didn't have a firm policy on tech distractions. Now, I address appropriate and inappropriate use on the first day. If I see repeated infractions, I discuss the matter privately with students. I have to ensure everyone's comfort.

If you are a habitual classroom texter, you'll have to be intentional about stopping. Put the phone in your backpack, leave it in your trunk—whatever you have to do. Otherwise, if you must have it (sick family member, children at home, etc.), then set your phone to vibrate and put it in your pocket rather than on your desk. If the text (or call) comes in, step out of class with as little noise as possible and take care of business. Don't linger outside of class; you may be counted as absent. Do not text under the desk (people can see you), and by all means, do *not* talk on your phone under the desk either (yes, students do this. Crazy!).

Now let's talk about other technology such as a laptop, Kindle, or iPad. I realize that many students dislike writing and prefer the efficiency, but with that efficiency comes temptation.

I am just as guilty. Put me in a training or meeting where a device is permitted, and I could easily veer away. When I'm writing for an extended period of time, I, too, drift to social media. It's true!

But, similar to texting, doing unrelated things on your laptop/device removes you from class. What if you're working on classwork? Isn't that okay? If your class gets "work" time, fine. Otherwise, getting ahead can put you behind if you miss the lecture or other pertinent information. Sometimes it makes sense to work in class to get your professor's review in the moment. But your first priority should be to engage in class.

Don't forget that, like texting, your laptop can distract others, particularly if you're using it for non-class-related things. If a classmate—or worse, your professor—sees you Facebooking or playing Candy Crush, this doesn't cast you in the best light. Would you want your boss or a colleague catching you? No!

Now, there are practical reasons to use a laptop in class, but you'll need to determine if you need the technology or if it is more of a hindrance. Also consider this: many articles in recent years suggest that students learn far more when handwriting notes. Google "Don't take notes with a laptop," and you'll find this article in Scientific American (and many more): http://www.scientificamerican.com/article/a-learning-secret-don-l-take-notes-with-a-laptop/. Think about if you might actually be weakening your ability to retain the material.

I don't want to make laptop or other device use in class sound all bad. It isn't. My student, Jackston, always brought his laptop, using it to follow the PowerPoint and to take notes. I could count on Jackston to do quick Google searches with me—me on the classroom computer, him on his laptop. We maximized our resources!

Ask Yourself This:

Why am I texting in class? Am I afraid I'll miss something, or am I intentionally distracting myself? Could my texts wait until after class?

and

Why am I bringing my laptop to class? Am I using it productively, or am I tempted to do other things? Am I willing to accept the consequences if technology distracts me from class?

Think This:

I should put my phone away while in class. If I see a text, I'll want to respond. I can text in an hour when class is over.

and

I will make a deal with myself to use my laptop only for classwork. Then I'll give myself an extra fifteen minutes of game time (or another reward). Anything I want to look up can wait until class is finished.

Not That:

I'll just respond real quick and say I'm in class.

One question, and your real quick text will turn into ten.

or

I'll check Facebook or Twitter for just a second.

There is no "just a second" with social media. Who are we kidding?

or

No one cares what I'm doing. It's my business.

True. But courtesy to your professor, those sitting around you, and even yourself, should also be your business.

Say This:

Before taking this advice, check your syllabus for a tech policy, or ask:

> Professor, what is your policy on technology use in class?

If you need to watch for a text or call, say:

> My mom needs me to possibly get my brother from school. She said she'd call or text me by eleven. If I have to step out of class for a minute, I wanted you to know why.

If your professor calls you out for texting or inappropriate laptop use, put it away immediately. After class, say:

> I made a mistake and didn't mean to be disrespectful. I'll use my laptop more responsibly/keep my phone out of sight.

(You can say the same thing to a fellow student who found your texting distracting.)

Not That:

> *I was only texting for a minute.*

A no-texting policy means no texting. Even for a minute.

or

> *Ooh, check out this website!*

Keep your surfing to yourself—or, better yet, stop!

or

I wasn't bothering anyone.

How do you know? Own up to it and then step away from the laptop (or at least close it).

The End Note

Many of us fool ourselves into thinking we can successfully multitask. The truth is that we may not want to accept that a situation requires our full attention.

Your professor must be the technology gatekeeper so everyone in the class is comfortable. Your laptop, phone, or other device shouldn't replace your classmates or your professor, even though you may want it to. Technology should support your education, not detract from it.

Seriously, I know how hard it can be to stay away from "other" business when you're in class. In order to break the habit, you need to reward yourself for doing so. And, of course, the reward can be—more screen time.

The Career Note

I know that there are more liberal policies in the workplace regarding texting at one's desk, using a laptop in meetings or other tech, etc. In some workplaces, being plugged in all the time is required. But I wondered, *What are the ramifications of technical distractions in the workplace?*

Interruptions and distraction have been studied in the software industry for decades. For programmers, it takes about ten to fifteen minutes after an interruption to rebuild the mental "context" required to make any additional progress. So, managing interruptions, even self-created ones, is critical. I've known people to quit jobs because they couldn't get anything done due to being constantly interrupted. Trying to juggle memory-intensive tasks like learning or programming just doesn't mix with anything that causes you to lose context—at least not if you want to do it well.

While nobody directly monitors social media usage anywhere I'd be willing to work, you have to realize that you have a finite amount of attention to spend. How you choose to spend your attention determines your intellectual and, most likely, professional life. The flip side is that you can't be concentrating all the time, either. You have to have a certain amount of "slack" in your day. However, you can't be haphazard about it. Plan it for when it's appropriate. Separate your concentration and your slack time. They don't mix well.

Ted, technology

23.

E-mailing Like a Professional, Part 1

What You Might Do:

Have the e-mail address Bootylicious775@xmail.com or send a message saying, "Hey Joe!"

What Your Professor Thinks:

Bootylicious775@xmail.com is not a professional e-mail address. I don't know who you are. And only my friends call me Joe.

The Real Story

Does your e-mail address look like one of these?

- thefourfortyfours@xmail.com

- catbite@xmail.com

- blackviper227@xmail.com

- Godschild@xmail.com

- vaginamacdonald@xmail.com

(Note: these are adaptations of real e-mail addresses.)

Or have you greeted your professor like this?

> Hey, Ellen!
>
> Yo, Ellen!
>
> How was your weekend?
>
> How 'ya doing?
>
> Luv, Student.

Maybe you've innocently e-mailed an offer to your professor for a free iPad. For every forward, you both get a chance to win.

Do students really use e-mail this way? They do. And it's time to kick the professionalism up a notch. Many notches.

The Backstory

Let's start with your e-mail address. Most students use addresses assigned by their campus, but even when that happens, students may not use an actual name. If the course management system is forwarding the e-mail, fortunately, the professor will see who it is from.

If your college allows you to designate your e-mail address, I can guarantee you that your professor isn't going to respond to a name she can't recognize (particularly when some students don't even sign their names at the end). Do you really want to be known as "bootylicious" or "catbite"? Also be careful about using all exclamation points, all Chinese letters, etc. Finally, your crazy e-mail address could end up in junk mail. Then you'll wonder why your professor didn't respond.

Bottom line: your professor and other campus staff need to be able to easily identify your correspondence. More importantly, college is a great opportunity to brand yourself, and your e-mail address is one of the first representations.

Once you've established your professional e-mail address, it's time to address your professor in the proper manner. Your professor is not your buddy. You may really like him or her, but you aren't "friends." Hence, the tone and nature of your e-mails should not be the same as with a friend or family member.

Professors should be viewed similar to a potential boss. Your professor may have a relaxed attitude and let you call her by her first name (you'll know on the first day), but that's still not an excuse to open with, "Hey, Mary!" You'll know immediately if you are being too casual by your professor's response.

Example:

You:

> "Hey, Mary,
>
> How are you doing? I hope you are having a great weekend. I'm doing well and I saw a great movie the other day. Went with my best friend and we had a great time.
>
> Hey, I have a question for you. Can you tell me when our journal is due?
>
> Thanks,
>
> Student"

And your professor's response:

> "Student,
>
> November 3, midnight.
>
> Thanks,
>
> Professor Jones"

Your professor certainly may wish you a good weekend, too, but remember: we get tons of e-mails—sometimes twenty to fifty per day. Many of us focus on answering your question or solving your problem rather than being chatty.

Speaking of being too casual; be careful about what you send to your professor. Most promotions, freebies, inspirational quotes, etc., happen on social media now. If, by chance, you receive something via e-mail and you think your professor must see it, just make sure the content is appropriate. Otherwise, the professor will wish you weren't cluttering her inbox.

Ask Yourself This:

Could my e-mail address give others a negative or questionable impression of me?

Does the tone of my e-mail sound like I'm talking to a friend or family member?

Is the content of my e-mail appropriate for my professor?

Think This:

College is business. I should have a professional e-mail address.

and

I can send my professor things related to the class, but otherwise, I should ask if he would mind if I send something else. I can be friendly without getting too personal or casual.

Not That:

I don't want to look in a bunch of places for e-mail. I hate e-mail.

E-mail is still the main form of communication in the workplace. Multiple e-mail accounts will be a part of your life for a while, so perfect time to get in the habit.

or

No one pays attention to e-mail addresses.

People do pay attention to unconventional addresses. You don't want the wrong attention.

or

My professor will like me more if I'm keeping it real!

Do your work, ask questions, be engaged in class. Your professor will appreciate you as a professional!

or

I really want get my professor that free pound of coffee!

Let your professor do e-mail forwards for her own freebies, if she so chooses.

Say This:

To your college help desk/IT department, if you don't already know this information:

Does the college give students e-mail addresses? Do I have to sign up, or is it automatically assigned to me? Where does the e-mail from my course management system go? Does all official college correspondence go to this e-mail?

To your professor if you sent an e-mail from an unknown e-mail address:

I e-mailed you on Wednesday and accidentally left my name off. You may not have been able to figure out that it was me from my e-mail address. I changed my address to my name. Would you like me to resend the e-mail?

Here are renditions of actual student e-mails that were done well:

Example #1:

> *"Dear Ellen* (which is what I ask my students to call me),
>
> *I hope you had a good weekend.* (A brief casual intro is fine if you don't overdo it).
>
> *I debated if I was going to send this assignment for review early, but came to the conclusion that it can't hurt. :)* (Student shows some personality here without being inappropriate. Gets to the point very quickly.)
>
> *Please let me know if I am way off base in what you are expecting from this assignment* (assertive statement saying what the student wants me to do).
>
> *Thanks.* (Fine way to close!)
>
> *First Name* (I know this student well)."

Example #2:

> "*Hi Prof. Bremen* (not terrible to say "Hi" if you know the professor),
>
> *I took your class in fall quarter last year, and I have an incomplete. I'm ready to finish the workload and would like to meet with you* (states problem and need).
>
> *As always, thank you for your patience.* (A kind close—personal but not uncomfortable).
>
> *Student"*

Example #3:

> "*Ellen Bremen* (my full name, even though this student and I had plenty of interactions, and first name would have been fine),
>
> *I have attached my current outline. I am not submitting this at this time for grading, but if you have extra time for a proofread, I appreciate it. I think it looks good. When I write, I have to put it down for a few hours and come back to make things the way I want.* (Again, gets right to the point and adds some personal note about the process, which is fine).

I have a couple of questions about format: specifically, is a .docx acceptable for the course management system?

You respond to e-mail more than any other teacher I know, and you do so with effective replies, not further confusion. I'm a busy parent, too, and appreciate the time you take for our class. (Always nice to have a compliment about what you appreciate, but not necessary if you can't say anything sincere.)

Thank you,

Student"

And finally, if you absolutely want to send your professor something unrelated to class, like a deal of some sort, just ask in person. Say:

Professor, I know you like chocolate. I saw a Groupon for the one you like. May I send it to you?

Your professor may say:

I'm on a chocolate fast, but thank you.

Don't take offense.

If you want to invite your professor to something (performance, etc.), also ask first:

I am in a theater production this weekend. I'd be glad to send you the information.

or

I thought I'd let you know that I'm in a play down-town this weekend, if you enjoy going to the theatre. Thanks for reading, and no need to respond.

Again, don't be upset if your professor doesn't bite. All professors have different comfort levels with fraternization.

Huge caution: be careful about offering discounts from work or anything that could be perceived as a bribe. There are ethical lines about this sort of thing. Wait until your professor is no longer your professor.

Of course, if you have some great content related to class, say:

Professor, I saw a video on YouTube that I think really fits what we're talking about this week. Here's the link. I hope you find it as interesting as I did.

Not That:

Would you please come to my play?

You don't want to make your prof uncomfortable. Always consider if what you say could be perceived as crossing a boundary. If in doubt, don't send.

And here is an e-mail that needed a redo:

"Hey, Ms. B! (Did I say casual?)

What's up today? (Do they really want to know?)

i missed the two people i was going to evaluate, is there any way i can make that up? maybe by doing two extra next time? (Aside from lack of capitalization, college work usually doesn't happen with negotiation.)

You are my fave! (Ugh! Remember what I said about sincere?)

(no signature)" (Ugh times two! Who is this from? Especially with an e-mail like jeanspocket220!)

The End Note

If you change your e-mail address, update your college record and change the forwarding e-mail in your course management system. You want your new professional e-mail address to actually get messages to you.

As far as being fun or cute in e-mail, remember that you don't have to be on your professor's good side to get a good grade. Do solid work.

The Career Note

I was interested to learn about e-mail habits important to cultivate for the workplace. I also wondered how prevalent e-mail is in industry, despite such widespread use of IM and texting:

Here are some tips:

E-mail is a permanent record, so take time to get it right. When writing to a professor or manager, be professional. Their perception of you is based on your tone.

E-mail can be forwarded, so never write anything that you don't want the world to see. If you forward an e-mail, check the whole chain before sending it to others.

E-mail should never be written when you are mad (you will almost always regret what you wrote). Don't put anything on the To: line—just write and save it. It will make you feel better but won't get sent.

If you are upset with your professor/coworker or manager, e-mail is not the way to work out issues. A face-to-face is warranted. Use e-mail to document the conversation after so each party has a record of what was discussed, or use it to send a thank-you for the great conversation.

I do not see e-mail slowing down in the workplace; many people rely on it too much. Now for important matters, or to get my attention quickly, I tell my employees to text me with anything urgent. E-mail gets buried in my inbox, and I can miss important e-mails very easily. Same advice for IM/ texting: either can be screen captured and sent all around. I have seen that happen, and folks are very upset that the other person did that. Often, it is just easier to work out issues/solve problems face to face."

Judy, aerospace

24.

E-Mailing Like a Professional, Part 2: Anger, Frequency, Responding

What You Might Do:

Send hate e-mail after receiving a poor grade (or over another issue), repeatedly e-mail, or fail to respond to your professor.

What Your Professor Thinks:

Flaming e-mails are a permanent record. E-mailing me ten times doesn't make me respond any faster. I've taken the time to e-mail you. Have the courtesy to respond.

The Real Story

Here are more variations of e-mails received from students:

11:29 p.m.:

"Dear Ellen,

I really need help with my assignment. I realize it's due in a half hour, but I hope you can get back to me.

Thanks,

Student"

And again at 12:15 a.m.:

"Dear Ellen,

I'm late now. Can I have an extension?

Thanks,

Student"

And at 1:45 a.m.:

"Dear Ellen,

I guess I'm not going to hear from you tonight, but I still have questions.

Student"

Then 2:35 a.m.:

> "Dear Ellen,
>
> I hope I'm not going to have a late penalty because I had questions and didn't get them answered in time to turn in the assignment.
>
> Thanks,
>
> Student"

Now I might respond:

> "I needed more notice to help you, rather than right before the assignment was due. It is unrealistic that I will be up through the night to answer questions. Next time, tell me that you are struggling earlier so I can give you help and in enough time."

Then, another e-mail:

> "Ellen,
>
> This is BS. It's not my fault that I couldn't ask the questions sooner. This really sucks that you won't give me an extension when I'm already struggling. Aren't you supposed to care about students?
>
> Student"

My response?

> "Student,
>
> I know you are frustrated, but this is escalating in an uncomfortable way. If it continues, I'll have to include my division chair in our conversation. Let's solve the problem instead. When would you like to come to my office?
>
> Ellen"

And what's the opposite of inflammatory e-mails? Students who never respond at all:

> "Dear Student,
>
> You're on my roster, but I haven't seen you since the third week. I'm concerned. If this term didn't work, withdraw from the course by the drop date to avoid a 0.0. I don't want the failing grade to hurt your transcript. Let me know if I can answer any questions.
>
> Ellen"

Crickets

And another:

> "Hello, Student,
>
> I tried to open your outline, but the format won't work. I'd like to give you feedback. Can you please attach a copy in .doc, .docx, or .rtf?
>
> Thanks,
>
> Ellen"

Again, crickets. This student received a poor outline grade and *then* responded, huffily: "But I sent you my outline and asked you to review it!"

Hand slap to forehead.

The Backstory

In this chapter, I want to talk further about e-mail content and process. My first tip? No angry e-mails! Your college has a student code of conduct. Your nasty e-mail is a permanent record and could have serious consequences. You don't need a new problem: disciplinary action. The short-term satisfaction is not worth the potential for disaster.

When you are so angry, look inward first. Could you have done something differently? If your professor is the problem, explain yourself professionally, specifically, and tactfully. You can assert yourself directly without tearing the other person down.

Conflict management is an art worth enhancing in college. In the workplace, harsh e-mails to a supervisor or anyone else could get you fired. Channel your feelings in the proper way.

Another idea: change the medium! A face-to-face or phone meeting won't escalate in the same way. Write down what you want to say to keep you on track.

My last suggestion: don't let anger cause you to "mass e-mail" or go up the hierarchy in the wrong way. I'll talk about this in Chapter 33, but realize that going above your professor's head won't necessarily solve the problem. I had a student who e-mailed my division chair, the vice president, president, *and* director of human resources because of a C. The HR director referred the student back to me and the division chair (which is typical; if the problem wasn't resolved, then the student could go up the chain).

Let's shift to another annoying e-mail habit: multiple messages when your professor doesn't quickly respond.

Professors are expected to give 24/7 service on e-mail. Many are on all the time, but if the policy is a twenty-four-hour response time, a faster response is a bonus.

A professor's time in class is actually the "shortest" part of his/her job. Here are other possible duties:

- Teach classes at different times (grading, building curriculum, etc.).

- Plan schedules, examine department/division policies, come up with programs, analyze exams. Lots of meetings!

- Serve students/advisees.

- Serve on campus committees (required in many professor's contracts). More meetings!

- Maintain professional involvement in organizations/advisory boards. Possibly researching/prepping conference papers, serving on the board, etc.

- Contribute to and attend campus events.

- Community involvement/service. Contractual obligation at some colleges.

These duties, and more, can require layers of work. Then there's e-mail management—its own job. In an hour, I can receive twenty-three e-mails.

Don't assume your professor is ignoring you. There aren't firm rules for response times, but look in your syllabus or ask the professor. If it's twenty-four hours *after* that, follow up to see if your original e-mail was received. If your professor never responds to e-mail (which does happen), then it's time for a face-to-face office visit. Still no response? This is a time to go higher (see Chapter 33).

Your professor may not respond to e-mails at night or on the weekend. Plan ahead. Also, try to solve the problem yourself first: look at the course management system, your syllabus, etc. In the workplace, you'll want to show that you can tackle issues yourself and that you seek help for the things that matter. So, if you are struggling to find good research, go to a librarian. Unsure about your paper's clarity? Read it aloud before you ask your professor (or ask a skilled person to review it).

Finally, always e-mail if your situation is personal. Don't use a discussion board. But if your question is general, post it so your professor can avoid answering fourteen individual e-mails.

One last quick tip: before accusing your professor of not re-sponding, make sure you are checking the correct inbox and that the college has the right e-mail address.

Before we leave this topic entirely, let's talk about the op-posite side of the e-mail issue: when you don't respond to a professor's e-mail.

Your professor may contact you if he's confused about an assignment submission, if he can't open your file, or if he is concerned about you. There are many professors who care to check in if you suddenly stop coming to class.

Always respond to your professor's message! Show your appreciation by hitting "Reply" rather than "Delete."

Most students don't respond because they don't know what to say. Be courageous; own up so you can get help. If your professor says you have a broken file, missed assignment, etc., solve the issue. Some students defend themselves: "I submitted it!" rather than resending.

Ask Yourself This:

Why am I e-mailing? Have I tried to find the information first? If I'm e-mailing again, how much time have I allowed for response? Did I leave myself enough time for help, or did I procrastinate? Should my issue be discussed face to face instead?

or

Why am I ignoring my professor's message? What's the worst that will happen if I respond?

Think This:

I may feel angry in college sometimes. Sending an e-mail that can make me look bad isn't worth it.

and

"I need to let my professor respond to my e-mail, based on his policy.

And if the professor e-mails you:

I'll respond. The professor cared enough to check in with me.

Not That:

My professor deserves exactly what I have to say!

Respectful assertiveness solves issues, not anger.

or

She should be more available for last-minute problems.

Your professor is responsible for responding within a timeline. You are responsible for getting help early.

or

My professor should just leave me alone. Can't she take a hint that I didn't e-mail back?

Many professors would leave you alone. This one cared to reach out.

Say This:

Professor, I didn't see an e-mail response time in your syllabus. Do you respond over the weekend? How early should we e-mail with questions?

(if your professor offers this).

If you haven't heard back within the response time, forward the original e-mail and add:

Professor, I e-mailed you yesterday at 2:00 p.m. I know you usually respond within twenty-four hours. I'd like to move forward on the assignment.

And if you are upset, say:

I am feeling very frustrated about this situation, and I'd like to discuss it, rather than apply blame or flame.

In response to your professor's message,

I appreciate you checking on me. This turned out to be a hard term for me. I will withdraw the class by the right date and see you hopefully next term.

or

This class was not the right fit. I will drop so I won't get a 0.0. I appreciate the reminder.

You can also be specific:

I found the online course too confusing and think I'm better off in the classroom.

And if there's a problem with your work:

Thanks for telling me that you couldn't open the file. Here's a new one in a different format. Would you confirm with me that you were able to open it?

Not That:

> Professor, your grading is totally out of whack. I worked hard! I don't know if you're tired, or grading too many papers, or what, but I am so mad!

"You" language has blame all over it. Focus on solving the problem instead with words that are assertive but respectful.

or

> I need you to answer this e-mail now!

or

> If I don't do well on this assignment, it will be because you didn't get back to me.

And finally, if your professor sends you an e-mail, I have no "**Not That.**" *Anything* you say will be better than ignoring the e-mail. Saying nothing sends a message, too—and sometimes, it's the wrong message.

The End Note

Some colleges are using texts and other media because many students don't like e-mail and won't read or respond to it. I can't emphasize enough that as of this book's print date (2016), e-mail is still a primary tool of communication in business. In college, e-mail serves as an official channel—something that social media or texting can't fulfill.

Don't abuse e-mail. Instead, use it to expand productive and positive communication with your professor.

Believe me, your excellent e-mail habits will be recognized and greatly appreciated!

The Career Note

What does an e-mail error look like in the workplace? Here's an example:

> I have had overly pushy candidates who I have given very specific instruction on when I was going to hire and the criteria they need to have met before I could set them up for an interview. This one candidate did not feel I was moving quickly enough. I was waiting for her to take the state exam and was waiting for the state to process her paperwork. She sent my manager an e-mail telling her she had contacted me but wanted answers soon. A little pushy. I did not appreciate that tactic, but she was willing to do anything and everything to get her foot in the door. My manager handed me her e-mail and laughed when I showed her my correspondence with this candidate.
>
> Teresa, healthcare

25. Making Fun of Professors on Social Media

What You Might Say:

(Absolutely anything and everything about your professor—see the examples below).

What Your Professor Thinks:

I bet you thought I'd never see that. But I did.

The Real Story

I love roasting professors on evaluations!

The professor asked me why I chose the topic for my paper. I said, "The deadline."

Why would the professor say he has a contact for me and then not give me *any* information?

We're not all vegetarians, Madame Nutrition Professor. Stop pushing it.

Why is my math professor in his car sleeping?

Pipe-cleaner art in communication class. Dominos in math class. Why am I in college again?

These are based on real social media updates from real students. Need I say more?

The Backstory

For professors who care about their reputation, the days of being concerned with students simply saying negative things to other students have pretty much ended. The ante is raised with social media, and I'm sure that's no surprise. If students put their whole lives out there for everyone to see, why not share all the thoughts and feelings about classes, too?

This is a bad idea for a million reasons. The most obvious is that your professor could see what you've written. Even if you are not connected to your professor in a social forum, you never know who will be. Another student? Another professor? Word could get back that you've said snarky things, and then your relationship with your professor may become strained.

Why should I care about that? you might think. *I didn't like him anyway.*

You never want to burn any bridges. You just never know when or if you will encounter that professor again. Also, just because you don't like the professor in this moment in time doesn't mean your feelings won't change. I had an entire 8:00 a.m. class once, the majority of which couldn't stand me. There were myriad issues in the class to begin with, combined with me being fairly new and not handling things as well as I should have. I did some major repair in that class, and a number of the students ended up taking other classes with me. Can you imagine if social media existed at that time? I can't even fathom what students would have said about me. And then, for those who ended up liking me after all, their comments would have already left a social imprint.

Consider this: if you are willing to say unkind things about your professor, your classmates, college, etc., then those words send others a message about *you*. Others may find your words funny. They may even agree with you, but in the back of their minds, you'll be that person who is willing to call someone out on social media. You're the person who will freely say negative things. The person reading your updates will think to themselves, *Will I be next? What would she say about me?*

Another thing to consider: even if you don't say anything negative about your professor, if you say things that reveal your work ethic, that could backfire on you. If you constantly post updates that you work last minute on assignments, that you're late to class—what will a potential employer think about that? What will someone who could network you into a job think about it?

Finally, unless you completely lock down your social media account (which isn't really possible with a little something called "screenshots," right?) what if you connect to future bosses or colleagues? You and I both know that it's tempting to scroll through past updates to get a fuller picture of our new friend, follower—whatever. Again, think about the impression that someone else would have of you based on your updates. If they are constantly negative or sarcastic, either toward yourself, your professor, or with respect to anything involving college, that could impact you in a negative way.

My suggestion is simple: think hard about what you are posting, in every social medium. Go back through your feed while you are in college to make sure there isn't something questionable that could bite you in the rear end later. If your social profiles and posts don't reflect the person you are in real life, then edit those social profiles, change your privacy levels (nothing is really private, though), and clean up your digital footprint.

Before I leave this section, I want to twist this subject a bit: there may come a time when a professor may do exactly what I'm warning you not to do. That's right: you may see unkind posts about things that students have done or are doing. Unfortunately, in these digital times, this is the way that many professors release frustration. These faculty believe that no student will ever see the comments because, after all, they are only being shown to the faculty's people. Have you seen national news about professors and employees in other industries finding themselves in trouble over social media misconduct? If you encounter this, then you have the right to report it.

Ask Yourself This:

> *Why am I motivated to say things about my professor, my classes, or my college on social media? Does it make me feel important? In control? Am I willing to accept the potential consequences of these actions?*

Think This:

I deserve to have a reputation for being a professional while in college. This is the time to cultivate that reputation. I don't need to ruin it just because of a few posts, tweets, etc.

Not That:

No one other than the people I'm connected to will ever see what I post.

Privacy isn't guaranteed on social media. If you wouldn't want someone to see it or if the information would hurt others' opinions of you, save yourself the trouble and don't post.

Say This:

If you want to post about your classes, here are some things that would put you in a positive light:

- What you've learned on a given day

- People you feel lucky to have met

- Events you've attended at your college

- Something you're proud of academically

- Upcoming events at your college

And on the off chance you find out that your professor is posting negative things about you or your class and this upsets you, you have the right to go to a department/division chair and say,

> Is there a policy about professors saying negative things about students/classes on social media?

(And then show what you've seen).

Not That:

I have the right to post what I want.

It's true. You do. Just make sure you're willing to deal with any potential repercussions and others' perceptions. Posting something snarky or inflammatory may feel really satisfying in the moment, but ask yourself if the cost of your online reputation is worth it.

The End Note

Here is another tweet that I saw recently: "Someone showed my professor my tweets on Twitter. She's going through my TL right now reading these tweets out loud."

Can you imagine if this happened in the classroom? If your professor went through your timeline, what would your tweets say about you?

One other note of caution, and I'll bring this up again in the chapter regarding classroom distractions: it's one thing to post negative updates on social media and another to do them while you are in class. Both are equally bad, but the latter is horrible, particularly if you get caught.

A version of this actually happened in my class: my students had some open work time to edit their outlines, and a student was using her laptop. As she was showing me her changes, sure enough, she had Facebook open, and I could see her crafting an IM to a friend about her "ridiculous professor." I could only surmise that I was the ridiculous professor, and I have to tell you, I was almost paralyzed to even help her after that. The only reason I didn't say anything was because her grandmother, who lived in the household, suffered a heart attack shortly after that class, and the timing never seemed right. Given the fact that I worked with her on absences and getting caught up again after caring for her grandmother, hopefully I wasn't so ridiculous anymore. This situation happened a number of years ago, but I never forgot about it, nor would I forget that student. I'm not recalling her in a positive way, particularly since she never gave any impression of frustration with me or my class. Do you see the perceptual dilemma here?

This may seem like a really "old" thing to say, but when e-mail was becoming big (sad that I remember this, but I do!), the big warning was: "Never write something in e-mail that you wouldn't want to see on the front page of the paper."

E-mail may be marginally less popular, and the newspaper, sadly, even less so, but that suggestion? #Truth.

The Career Note

I went back to the author of the bestselling book, *A World Gone Social*, and asked: "What is your perception of bashing professors on social media? How does this correlate to building proper social media etiquette for the workplace?"

> *In the Social Age, everything we say online is open to scrutiny. And we all have nearly equal access to everything said. Think your professor (or parents, boss, or mentor) isn't on Facebook, Snapchat or Yik Yak? You could be wrong. And what you said could be found.*

This issue, of course, goes beyond your inner circle. In fact, recruiters and employers have made social snooping an art form. If they see your social profiles contain negative comments—from seemingly innocent to more inflammatory—they will take note. They'll see you are more focused on the problem rather than the solution. And they'll choose to interview someone else for that internship or job you really wanted.

Social media etiquette isn't just for those already in the workforce; it's for everyone that hopes to someday build a solid professional reputation. Be a good digital citizen now. The professional side of you will thank you later.

Mark, social media/business consultant

Building a Relationship with Your Professor/Other Campus Resources

26. Using Office Hours to Your Advantage

What You Might Say:

I didn't come to your office because I thought you'd be too busy.

What Your Professor Might Think:

My office hours are scheduled so I can be busy working with students like you.

The Real Story

I don't understand this assignment!

I am frustrated over my grade!

I want to learn more about the communication major and what types of jobs I can do.

I am having a terrible quarter and need some advice.

These are all reasons students visited my office in the past year. If you want to enhance your possibilities for assistance and advice, seeing your professor in real time is the way to go.

The Backstory

Whether you are working with a professor, teaching assistant, etc., most colleges require faculty to hold office hours for student, staff, and even community members' visits. The times/days of these office hours are often public and can sometimes be found on the college website (in addition to your syllabus). I can't encourage you enough to know your professor's office hours and use them!

You may wonder, *Why can't I just e-mail or text? Seeing my professor is going to be uncomfortable! Just her and me in that office. No, thanks!*

Whether you need to problem-solve or seek a stronger professional relationship, you only stand to benefit by going to your professor's office hours from time to time. Before I talk about how to have a productive meeting, let's go behind the scenes.

Every college requires faculty to hold a certain number of office hours. This is based on the professor's work contract. My college requires five hours per week; other colleges may be more or less. A professor can usually select the days/times, and ideally, ones that work for students.

Many professors put in numerous unofficial office hours to complete class/college-related work (think committee reports, report writing, curriculum building, etc.). Some professors even hold virtual office hours (Skype or similar programs), particularly if they teach online or from out of state. Again, your syllabus should provide information about where/how office hours occur.

Your professor's office hours are typically drop-in and first come, first served. If you have a specific problem or question, make a dedicated appointment. You can do this via e-mail, in person, or by locating your professor's office phone number on the syllabus or campus website. Making an appointment means you won't be at the mercy of others who stopped in first, whose visits may be lengthy.

When you schedule an actual meeting, you allow your professor to work around their possible campus conflicts, such as meetings, or personal obligations (picking up their children, meeting a commuter carpool, etc.). Some professors need to factor in travel time if they're teaching at different campuses.

Likewise, tell the professor if you only have a certain time window so she knows what time constraints you're working with, too. If you can't make any of your professor's scheduled office hours, find out what other times might be available.

On occasion, your professor may not be in her office, even during posted hours. Sometimes we attend meetings or have other on-campus obligations during office hours; however, some professors leave a note on their door, or a department/building admin person (think secretary) might advise when they'll return. If the professor uses a course management system, they might e-mail saying that office hours are changed/canceled.

Now let's focus on what to do before your meeting. Prepare any documentation you need for your meeting. Have a question about an assignment, grade, or something class related?

Make sure the documentation is easily accessible. You don't want to use up precious time hunting through your backpack or frantically searching your laptop. Also, just like if you were going to a doctor's visit, write your questions down in advance. This is excellent practice so you don't become flustered and forget something important.

Once in your professor's office, you may exchange quick, casual conversation ("How's it going today?"), but be clear about why you are there. You may feel nervous, but remember: your professor is a human being, and you are a human being. This professor is simply a work partner (who happens to give you a grade) and, really, both of you are on the same team.

Be yourself, and be friendly without being over the top. You don't need to compliment the professor or ask questions about things you see in their office (pictures, artifacts, etc.), unless you are genuinely interested. We can all recognize insincerity, right? Try to maintain direct eye contact, a relaxed posture, and no checking phones during the meeting, unless you have an emergency (and then say so).

If you are upset, try to stay calm. Anger may make you feel better in the moment, but you don't want fury to become the problem to solve rather than the problem itself.

Speaking of problems, I won't get into typical problem-solving conversations in this chapter (ones related to your class) because the other thirty-plus chapters will help with those. Here are some other things you can discuss with your professor:

- Research interests

- Why your professor got into teaching/their field

- Other classes you might want to take in the discipline or classes that are complimentary for your degree

- Jobs in the field unrelated to teaching

- Why your professor chose their university/recommendations for universities with strong programs in their field

Aside from discipline-specific questions, sometimes your professor can help with other college issues. They can't intervene, but they might be able to help you find the right staff person in financial aid, registration/records, counseling, etc. Some professors will even call faculty in other divisions to help you network or to ask how quickly their waitlists move. Not every professor is willing to do these things, nor are they able. But tell your professor if you have a broader campus question/problem and see if they'll offer advice.

Ask Yourself This:

What stops me from using my professor's office hours? If I have a problem, would I feel intimidated to go? What benefits might I have if I visit my professor in her office?

Think This:

I should view my professor's office hours as a way to expand my possibilities for assistance and advice.

Not That:

I will e-mail my professor if I need anything. I'll feel more comfortable that way.

E-mail is fine to set an appointment. Otherwise, remember that a lot of communication can be missed or misinterpreted in writing. Also, you remove the possibilities for other types of beneficial conversations.

If you want to set a meeting:

> I see that your office hours are Tuesday and Thursday, 12:00–3:00 p.m. I'd like to meet with you Thursday and want to make sure you are available.

Then add the reason why:

> I need help with our next assignment.

> *or*

> I am wondering if you can tell me about jobs in the field.

> *or*

> I am having an issue and was wondering if you could give some advice.

Some professors are using tools like You Can Book Me (https://youcanbook.me/) to schedule office hours online. Both of you will receive reminders, but you can let your professor know if you booked a meeting this way: "I look forward to seeing you for our meeting that I scheduled at 3:00 p.m."

Critical: however you make an appointment, be 95 percent sure that you can make it! Say:

My schedule is clear, but if something comes up and I cannot make this appointment, how should I get in touch with you?

Be open about constraints (e.g., childcare, your job, or potential traffic) if you are leaving for the college at a different time than usual.

Also, confirm the meeting; e-mail is fine for this. Say, "I have an appointment scheduled with you tomorrow at 2:30. Just making sure this still works."

Then, be on time, and your professor should hopefully not leave you waiting either. Remember that if you are meeting right after your prof's class, she may be asking post-class questions. Give him/her about fifteen minutes, and then leave a note with your phone number if she still doesn't show.

If you have to leave work or deal with complex scheduling, say:

I am going to take off from work an hour early so I can make this appointment.

or

I have to get a babysitter in order to meet you.

This way, the prof will know that she shouldn't let any issues get in the way of meeting *you*.

Do everything you can to keep the appointment. If a crisis arises, e-mail quickly and back up with a phone call to voice mail. You can also ask the campus operator to help you locate the building admin (in other words, the secretary), and you can leave a message with that person, too.

If you forgot the appointment, apologize:

I'm sorry that I missed my appointment with you. I will not let this happen again.

You may want to just use the professor's office hours next time or make another appointment, but by all means, be there. Two no-shows would be, well, let's just say, very bad.

Not That:

It doesn't matter if I try to see the professor; she's never there, anyway!

Tell the professor after your next class, "I have tried to come to your office three times during office hours and seem to be missing you. I need to meet with you. What would be a good time to do that?"

You can also ask the department/building secretary, "When is Professor Jones usually in her office? I've tried to see her three times, and the office is always dark. Do you recommend another way to get in touch with her?"

When you do meet with your prof and need a follow-up, say, "I would like to come back. What times are you generally here, because I must have missed you during office hours a couple of times?"

If you find that you habitually cannot find prof during office hours, note this on your student evaluation.

The End Note

Nothing replaces face-to-face conversation with your professor, plain and simple. You need the practice of having professional conversations. Your professor can offer that practice. Take it!

The Career Note

I wanted to interview someone who promotes the development of genuine relationships. My industry professional does this via *ReturnonRelationship.com* and his hashtag #RonR. I asked, "What advice would you give for students who are less comfortable connecting with professors and other campus staff, face to face, in their offices?"

The benefits of being comfortable with face-to-face interaction are evident in everything we do, from family interactions, to workplace effectiveness, to travel—and the ability to work with people in any situation we may encounter. The best time to start developing this ability is while attending college in a relatively "safe" environment, where making mistakes is not only expected but can even be encouraged. College professors, first and foremost when presenting themselves in the advisory role, allow every student the opportunity to hone their engagement skills with someone who perhaps does make them nervous. Exercising their relationship-building muscles when under a bit of stress is a good thing, since this will often be the case for many when engaging with people of status and influence, but the professor is a safe zone. Professors need to make this known, help students to understand the benefit, and encourage them to reach out regularly without fear of the inevitable mistakes and missteps. Relationships are like muscle tissue—the more they are engaged, the stronger and more valuable they become.

Ted, social media/brand strategy

27. Requesting a Letter of Recommendation

What You Might Say:

I need a letter of recommendation. It's due in two days. I realize I wasn't your best student, but I'd really appreciate it.

What Your Professor Thinks:

I would have been perfectly willing to help you with this—with some notice.

The Real Story

Loraleah was finishing the end of her academic term and hadn't ever made any connections with her profs. She really didn't think she had to, since her grades were strong and she didn't usually require a lot of help.

Suddenly, Loraleah found herself applying to a program that required a letter of recommendation. Loraleah felt a little weird about asking, so she put off the request. Before she knew it, her application package was due. She couldn't turn it in incomplete, so she had no choice but to find a few profs and ask them to help her out.

Let's say that Matteo applied to that same academic program. His profs knew him all too well because he struggled a lot to keep his GPA where it was. Even with his work, he still fell somewhere between a 2.5 and 3.0, depending on the class. Matteo almost felt like he shouldn't bother asking for a letter of recommendation. Only A students should get those.

The Backstory

I can't tell you how many students like this I see over the course of a year. Recommendation letters are one of the biggest reasons to connect and network with your profs. So many students skip that opportunity, only to realize months or even years later that they could really use a prof's unique validation of their work. Then, students typically e-mail saying, "I'm not sure if you remember me, but ..."

I've been teaching for fifteen years, and it's impossible to remember every single student I've ever had, though, of course, I remember many of them. When a student e-mails after a year or so has gone by, I often have to scramble to research the student's work. If your college uses a course management system, as most do, often those change every few years. While the college archives student records and course management system files, these aren't readily available to profs if the system has already changed to something new. Once I have a good handle on who the student was and how they did in my course, only then can I construct a recommendation letter that will represent them in the best light. If that student had only requested the letter upon exiting my class, I could have written a stronger letter, one that captures specific examples of their work (which is what will make them memorable for a college application or an employer).

Now let's take Matteo's example. So many students believe that they don't deserve a recommendation letter if they don't have a high GPA. I want to tell you right now that regardless of your performance, unless you were a complete disruption and menace to the instructor and the class, there is no reason you can't have a recommendation letter.

Think about this: grades are a snapshot of performance over a limited period of time. They are important but do *not* always tell the entire story. I recommend that you pick a few classes where you exhibited strong work ethic, even if your grades missed the mark. Maybe you contributed a ton to class discussion. Maybe you took your prof's feedback but couldn't get past a funky grading scheme. Maybe you studied your ass off but felt sick on the day of a test, and that test brought your grade down a letter. In these situations, your prof could likely have more to say about you than the final outcome.

One thing you could do is go back and look at your syllabus and assignments from your class. If you can't find the syllabus, it may be online, or you could ask an administrative secretary for the building or department to locate one for you. Then, make an "I did" list: Did you have a group project? How did you perform in that project? What was your role? What were your papers about? Did you do speeches or other presentations? Make a list of your "other" outcomes from class. If you were the team leader in a group project, write that down. If you had a unique paper or speech topic, list that, too.

Some other notes: Did you have perfect attendance? Did you always engage in class discussion? Did you show up for class on time? Add this to your list.

Notice I'm not asking you to write down what your grades were. I'm asking you to write down what you did in the class.

Obviously, if you just had the class, then the information will be fresh in your mind.

I have one last recommendation for you, and it may come as a surprise:

There are some professors who may ask you to write the letter yourself. I disagree with students writing their own recommendation letters. Here's why: whoever wants that recommendation letter is seeking a perception of you in someone else's words. If you are writing your own perceptions of you and the prof is simply signing off, that's not very authentic. Calling out details of why you think you deserve the letter is fine, but it's another thing to undertake the task.

If your professor says, "Why don't you just write what you want and I'll sign it?" I would reply, "I understand you must be very busy. I would appreciate your words because I can learn from what you have to say. If this is not the right time to make this request, no problem." Then move on to another professor.

Hopefully, your professor will step up and you'll be golden. From there, have a clear follow-up plan. Arm your prof with details they need for the letter (i.e., whether you need a specific addressee or just something general). Make any deadlines clear (a two-week lead time, at least), and discuss how the prof can return the letter to you (E-mail? In person? Or does the letter need to be sent somewhere?).

Say This:

If you are still on campus, make an appointment with the prof or send an e-mail, saying:

Dear _____

"I am wondering if you would write a recommendation letter for me. I need the letter for _____ (Scholarship? Entry into a program? General letter for future opportunities?), and I feel that, based on the work in your class, you could speak well to my abilities. Here are a few things that stood out about my work for your course (then give examples)."

Sincerely,

If you didn't do so well in the course, say:

Dear _____,

"I didn't ace your class, but I definitely learned a lot from my experience. My final grade could have been better, but I did a number of other things that were positive. (e.g., 'I always enjoyed the discussions in our class and appreciated earning all of the possible participation points'). I can share what some of those things are. I understand you may have to decide if you feel comfortable supporting my request."

"My paper on the Yanomamo tribe taught me how to write a thesis statement and carry a topic through in a focused way. I lost points on that paper because my sources were weak. I realized I needed to work more closely with a librarian, and on my next paper, I did get help."

Sincerely,

Ask Yourself This:

What type of recommendation letter could a prof write for me? If I didn't get the best grades, did that happen because of laziness, procrastination, or disinterest?

If this is the case, you may not feel comfortable asking the prof to write anything for you, and your prof would feel equally uncomfortable.

The End Note

A student recently told me they were in a class where the prof was incomprehensible. Students complained, and grades suffered. I know that this student works very hard. Like I said, sometimes grades just don't tell the whole story.

You have abilities and qualities that can expand your story. You just need support in telling it.

Dear _____,

I am writing this letter to support Student in his/her quest for entry into X program.

I worked with Student during winter 2013 in my 200-level Interpersonal Communication course. In this course, I have unique opportunities to assess students' face-to-face and online communication. In class, Student heartily contributed to all of our discussions. I could always

---

count on Student to appropriately engage and advance conversations. Student supported and encouraged others' ideas, which I found impressive, particularly since this is important practice for successfully communicating in outside environments.

In the required discussion forums, Student aptly and accurately analyzed personal experiences in tandem with the theories we were studying. I noticed that Student always replied to other students' posts, acknowledging their thoughts and appropriately adding his/her own. This offered me a glimpse into Student's ability to interpersonally communicate in an online medium, and I felt that Student, once again, exhibited keen insights and above-average skill.

For our major paper, Student undertook the topic of how social media affects college students—this was after Student's own three-day social media/texting fast. Student conveyed thoughts in a focused manner and showed developing information-literacy skills.

As you know, grades do not always give the full picture of a student's ability. I definitely believe this to be the case with Student. Student can tell you about the outcome and changes made as a result. Reflecting on how one can improve and then taking action is an important skill. This quality just adds to Student's positive attributes that I hope you will consider.

(Continued)

> If I can answer other questions about my time working with Student, I would be glad to have that conversation.
>
> Respectfully,

Feel free to stop here, or read on to see an example of a letter that I would write for a student without an ideal grade:

The Career Note

I had one basic question: How can aligning with professors, seeking them out as mentors, etc. be positive for a future career? I realize this idea seems obvious, but I also wondered how this relationship can help a student prepare to work with a supervisor someday.

> *Professors have extensive experience and many contacts and can be instrumental in helping a student with little or no work experience find a first job. After the student lands her or his first job, the professor can be a great sounding board and source of career guidance. I have friends in their fifties and sixties who are still in touch with their professors from forty years ago.*
>
> *Aligning with a professor as a mentor helps a student in a future supervisor/employee relationship in at least two ways. The first is by providing an opportunity to practice interacting with a person in a position of power and authority. The second is that the mentor/mentee relationship doesn't end upon*

graduation, and the student has, in the mentor, a valuable resource upon which she or he can call for many years into the future. An example would be in the case of the student working for a difficult boss. In such a case, a mentor could prove extremely helpful in navigating the turbulent and sometimes dangerous waters of having a bad boss.

Don, customer service training/information technology

28. Getting Connected on Social Media

What You Might Say:

Do you have SnapChat? Instagram? Can we follow each other on Twitter or Facebook? Can we connect on LinkedIn?

What Your Professor Thinks:

I need to have social media boundaries while you are my student.

The Real Story

When I taught in Georgia, I was in the Publix frozen vegetable aisle, and my student, Josh, tentatively approached me.

"Ms. Bremen?"

"Hi, Josh! I didn't know you worked here."

"Yeah, about six months now."

Then Josh said, "Hey, can I ask you something? I need some help with my speech topic."

Josh saw an unexpected opportunity to get help. In the frozen peas. I should have felt happy that Josh was asking for help, right? But there are boundaries between professors and students. Seeing each other out and about around town would be one of them.

These days, boundaries are more blurred than ever with social media. You don't need to run into each other at the store. You're only as far as your laptop or phone! I learned this when, in 2011, I joined Facebook and Twitter. My personal policy was no friending or following of students until they weren't my student anymore. That became complicated when I set up a Facebook page for my blog/book. Then one of my students, Ranija, IM'd:

"Hi ... Can I ask you a question about my grade on the last paper?"

I replied, "Let's talk about this in my office tomorrow."

Ranija wished me a good night and said she'd see me then.

The Backstory

I *completely* understand why students wouldn't think twice about asking class-related questions of a professor via social media. If you are communicating with others largely through social media, logically, you'd seek to connect with your professor this way, too.

But I want you to think about that frozen veggie aisle at Publix or if you saw your professor out for dinner with her family. You may say a quick "hello," but you wouldn't tromp over and talk schoolwork.

Our obsession with social media has caused many colleges to implement policies around student–professor interactions. It's a double-edged sword, though, since colleges are using social media to connect with students because of how they can transmit information. When it comes to your professor and social media, consider some general best practices:

First, if your professor offers dedicated social media for your class (Instagram, Facebook, etc.), use it as intended. Your professor will guide you on parameters. Avoid any postings that involve your grades, reasons for not attending class, late work, etc. Save these discussions for an official channel (i.e., campus e-mail or the e-mail in your course management system). Both places are far more appropriate for you to say, "Professor Jones, I need to discuss a problem with you." Also, depending on the severity of the issue, you may need an in-office visit or phone call.

If your professor has relaxed social media policies (she will "friend" you while in her class, unrelated to school business), respect her privacy and be mindful of what you post. Do you really want your professor to see you partying? Or posting how exhausted you are at 1:53 a.m. when your class is at 8:00 a.m.? Probably not.

Despite your professor's policies, I strongly recommend avoiding *any* personal social media relationship until you are no longer in the student–professor capacity.

Twitter is a somewhat different story. With its 140 characters, the possibility is reduced for oversharing (this is totally dependent on the user, of course). On Twitter, your professor is likely to be connected to industry people, colleagues, etc.; they may tweet and retweet some valuable information. If Twitter holds popularity (as of this writing, that's questionable), it's incredibly useful for learning about your field, general career building, and networking. Your professor may have tips on other professionals to follow, but once out of her class, you can respectfully ask for networking opportunities or introductions.

Let's talk LinkedIn for a moment: LinkedIn connects your professional network to someone else's. Who wouldn't want to tap into their professor's network, right? And, it's all work related, which doesn't mar those personal boundaries.

I still recommend that you wait to link in with your professor. She may want to make sure the quality of your work and your work ethic is worth connecting to. Just being real here.

Ask Yourself This:

> What is my motivation for connecting to my professor on social media? Have I shown the kind of work ethic that would make my professor comfortable about connecting and/or sharing his network with me?

Think This:

> Unless my professor has a clear social media policy, I'm smart to wait until my grade has been calculated and the term is over before I make a request. Waiting will give me the chance to show that I'm someone worth staying in contact with or sharing contacts with.

Not That:

> I've read a lot of tips on getting on a professor's good side and getting them to notice me. What better way than on social media? It's like sitting in the front row, isn't it?

Connect with sincerity. I highly doubt any professor would say,

> Wow, Mila has an awesome Instagram, and she
> retweets me all the time. She's getting a C, but I'll
> give her a B.

And just so you know, your professor does not have to notice or like you. Most professors do not do business this way. You do not need to connect on social media in order to have a good working relationship. Have a strong work ethic. Do solid work. You and your prof will get along just fine—on and offline.

Say This:

*Before you take this advice, check your syllabus, the college website, or your student handbook for an official policy regarding student–professor social media use.

If your professor has a social media page in line with your institution's requirements, then say, "Professor, I see that you use social media in our class. If I have a grade-related question, should I use your e-mail instead?" Get the straight scoop about where your communication should happen before you make a social media flub.

If you are want to follow, friend, etc., and no policy exists, say, "Professor, I am on (insert social media) and am wondering if I can connect with you. Do you have a policy about this?" Never, ever just "follow" or "friend" without asking first, particularly if you are still in the student–professor relationship.

If your term ends and you want to connect with your prof, say, "Professor, I really enjoyed this class, and I would like to stay in contact with you. I am on (insert social media). Where would be the best place to connect with you?"

(Additional tip here: if your prof does connect with you via LinkedIn, it is appropriate to request an introduction to another one of his contacts. Always say why you are making the request: "I see your colleague has expertise in my area of interest. Could you make an introduction?")

If a term has passed since you've had your professor's class and you want to connect on LinkedIn, do not just send the generic invite! Send an e-mail saying, "Professor, I had your Intro to Communication class in Fall 2009. I was the student who did a speech on English Ivy (or some other identifying factor). I'm now at the University of Washington (or bring the prof up to speed on whatever you are currently doing), and I'd like to connect on LinkedIn. Can I send an invite?"

To connect on Twitter, say, "Professor, I notice you are on Twitter, and I could learn from your tweets about the field. I'd love to follow you. I'd also be interested in recommendations of other good accounts to follow."

Not That:

Can you give me some help with our upcoming class project?

on a non-college social media page. Even on a college-related page, make sure you are supposed to ask for help there.

The End Note

Interestingly, some students have their own social media boundaries: *they* won't even consider connecting with a professor until after a term is over.

So what happened to Josh?

Of course, I quickly helped refine his speech topic in the frozen foods. Josh followed up with a visit to my office.

I teach in a bigger city now; I rarely run into my students. I take great joy in maintaining contact with many former students via social media. I love following their professional happenings, seeing pictures of their families, etc. Students can contact me for a reference or college/career advice with ease, which is an upside to this medium.

Connecting with students, even after they are my student, has caused me to be mindful of everything I post. Because I'm older and didn't grow up with social media, I'm fine with this. Some of your professors might feel the same way.

Finally, think about your true motivation for connecting with your professors, whether you are tempted to do so during class or thereafter. Do you think they will like you more if you are connected on social media? Are you curious about your professor outside of the classroom? Do you feel like you'll get more help through a different channel? Are you genuinely interested in maintaining professional contact? Do you perceive your professor as someone who could be a friend after class ends?

As stated in other parts of this book, you don't need to get on your professor's good side through social media or otherwise, and you certainly don't need to have a personal connection in order to earn a good grade (which would actually cross significant ethical boundaries!). You may see real value in staying connected with your professor, either personally or professionally, and social media is a practical way to make that happen. Choose the proper channel for your continued contact. If in doubt, start with LinkedIn—the safe, professional choice—and go from there.

The Career Note

Who better than to ask the author of the best-selling *A World Gone Social* about benefits and drawbacks of students and professors connecting on social media?

We used to have clear lines of delineation; our work lives were clearly separated from our personal lives. Today, those lines have blurred so much we barely see them.

Bosses are Facebook friends with those they manage. Students and professors belong to the same LinkedIn Groups. Mentors and mentees participate in the same Twitter chats. We're all connected now, or soon will be.

There are benefits to these connections, of course. Among them are open dialogue on critical issues, a more collaborative approach to problem solving, a better sense of who the "whole" person is rather than just the person we are at work or school, and more.

The drawbacks are also present. Chief among them: the feeling that we've lost the private side of our lives and that we always have to be "on"—we can never just be ourselves.

But here's the reality: privacy in the Social Age is dead, or at least on life support. Once we become part of the social mainstream, we are vulnerable— whether we are official "friends" with our professors and bosses or not. So choose what you post

carefully. Assume what you do post will be seen by everyone. And the stuff you really don't want people to see—well, make sure it never gets online.

Because what happens in Vegas, stays in Vegas— until some dumbass puts it on Facebook.

Mark, social media/business consultant

SECTION 2

Won't Discuss—and May

Not Want You to Know

Dear Wonderful Reader,

Now that you've delved into the tips on how you can communicate more productively in common classroom situations, let's shift gears: students aren't the only ones who miscommunicate or say things in a clueless way. I couldn't write a book like this without also addressing that professors sometimes communicate unproductively, too.

I realize that when your professor bungles an interaction, you might feel powerless and intimidated. It is hard to stand up to someone who is evaluating your performance and who has authority. But here's the truth: your professor isn't always right, and you have the right to stand up for yourself, or at least inquire about an issue, when you have a concern or complaint.

In these next chapters, I will give you the real and backstories about mistakes professors may make, knowingly or unknowingly. I will give you the words to face these sometimes daunting situations and, hopefully, emerge from them with solutions and encouragement.

I want to emphasize that dealing with conflict or difficult situations is *hard*. I don't discount that fact. However, hard interactions can happen at any time. You can't run from them forever, and in the case of a college issue, failing to self-advocate in a positive manner can truly impede a successful outcome.

Even if you are terrified to confront one of these issues, try your best to find the strength to do it. Use friends, family, or others who care about you as support. You can vent to them before the conversation with your professor, and you can fall apart on them for relief when you've gotten through it. But more than anything, get the questions you need to get answered, and respectfully ask questions about issues that seem unfair, unjust, and unclear.

You've got this!

Ellen

29.
Knowing What Your Grades Mean/ Receiving Timely Feedback

What You Might Think:

I got a number (or letter) on this paper. I have no idea what I did right or wrong.

What You Have the Right to Say:

What does this number *(or letter)* mean?

The Real Story

"If you are going to give a student any less than 100 percent, you'd better have a reason why," said my graduate program advisor, once upon a time. I've never forgotten that advice.

Hence, you deserve to know what your grades mean, whether you've received a number or letter with no explanation or unclear suggestions for improvement. You may feel uncomfortable about questioning this, but your basic right as a student is to know how you are being evaluated.

The Backstory

If you have no idea what your grade or feedback means, my first tip is to try to find an associated checklist, rubric, or even the assignment description. That may help you figure out what went right or wrong before you ask for grade/feedback clarification.

You may wonder why professors are cryptic with feedback and grades. There's not a simple answer. Some professors grade very quickly—they have piles of papers and can only spend X minutes per item. They feel their number or letter grade should say it all. Other professors feel like students don't really read their comments or care about feedback. One professor told me, "I give a numerical grade, and if they want to know more, they can come see me." The professor added that, sadly, few do.

Fortunately, the majority of professors want you to do as well as they can take you and as far as you can take yourself. So, they load you up with feedback. But what about when you don't understand their comments?

You need to know. The feedback will help you identify a) how you are meeting the curriculum standards (remember those objectives from your syllabus we talked about earlier?) and b) how the professor grades your work.

Let's focus on b) and how the prof grades your written work (e.g., essays, research papers, etc.) Some professors are heavy-handed on mechanical errors (grammar, punctuation). Myriad errors could fail you, regardless of your paper's content. Other professors look only for errors that impede the paper's meaning. They'll suggest that you proofread more closely, but they won't necessarily reduce your score. You need to know what your professor is looking for and what standards should be met.

Find out what's required *before* your work is submitted. Again, look for a checklist, rubric, examples of high-quality student work, scoring sheet, etc., to help you compare what you have to what is required.

If your professor doesn't have samples, rubrics, etc., then ask, "Can you go over how we will be graded on this assignment?" Then take good notes on what the professor says. If the professor is vague, slow him down: "Can you give an example of what you mean?" We professors don't always know when we're being unclear!

When you receive your paper, you may receive the rubric or checklist along with it. If you don't, bring the checklist, rubric, etc., to the professor and say, "I used this when I worked on the assignment. Can you explain further what I needed to do differently?"

Or, if your professor says, "This part of your paper needs a stronger transition," ask what "stronger" means if you're unsure. Were there examples from class? If not, get clarification to accurately strengthen those transitions.

Now if you took a fixed-answer test, your professor doesn't have to tell you the correct answers. He may expect you to hunt those down yourself and, really, if you want to connect and retain the material, you should. Or tell the professor to lead you in the right direction if you have no idea.

Otherwise, on subjective work, get concrete tips to fix those issues, particularly if a similar assignment creeps up again.

One last note here: you should know your grade standing throughout the term. So many students rightfully complain, "I have no idea what my grade is!" because work hasn't been returned to them for weeks or maybe their professor isn't posting grades anywhere. Never wait until the end of the term to find out how you're doing. If your professor isn't regularly grading your work within a week (and there is no update), you'll need to ask questions. If you need the feedback/grade from the current work for a rapidly approaching assignment, you may need to ask the professor to change the deadline to accommodate for the grading delay.

Ask Yourself This:

Has my professor provided any samples, rubrics, checklists, or other information (i.e., "Here is what an A assignment would look like") so I know how I will be evaluated before I do this work? When I receive my grades back, do I usually understand why I received the grade I did? Do I feel scared to ask for specifics? Am I receiving my grades back in a reasonable timeframe?

Think This:

I have the right to learn how my work was evaluated. Otherwise, I may not know what my professor is looking for, and upcoming work could suffer.

Not That:

The professor gave me a 75. Not sure what that means. I only care about the number, anyway.

Don't sabotage yourself from improving. Don't cost yourself a higher grade next time.

Say This:

First, find any examples, checklists, rubrics, etc., that your professor provided. Bring this with you and say:

> Professor, I appreciate the information to show us what's required for this assignment. I want to do well, so I've reviewed it closely. I am confused on line ten in the rubric. Can you explain this?

If no documents exist, say:

> I'd like to do my best on this upcoming paper. Do you have examples, a checklist, or anything that would help?

Your professor may give you a verbal list, and you could offer to create a checklist for her! I bet she'd appreciate your initiative.

If you received an assignment with a number/letter grade and no feedback, say:

> I'd like some more specifics on what I could have done. Can you give me a few tips?

If you received a checklist, scoring sheet, rubric, etc., with your paper but you don't know what the item means, say,

> I thought I did _____ the right way, but I missed this one. Can you explain it further so I get it right next time?

If you received written feedback but can't understand what the feedback meant (even if you can't read the handwriting), say:

Professor, I appreciate you giving me suggestions, and I'd like to work on those for the next assignment. I see that you wrote _____, and I'm not clear on what that means. Can you give me an example?

In the above situation, a technique called "paraphrasing" would serve you well: repeat what the professor said in your own words:

I see your comment that I need to cite my sources more clearly. I think you're saying that the reader would need to know more information about the website/publication. Am I understanding this correctly?

Disclaimer #1: If your professor won't clarify the feedback (unusual!), then visit another professor in the same department. Many faculty use similar assignments. Avoid saying that your professor won't help. Instead, say: "I feel like I need another perspective on what I needed to do differently. I realize I'm not your student, but you teach this course. Do you have any tips?"

Don't worry about the other professor "tattling." Many professors help each other's students. It's fine.

Disclaimer #2: If you absolutely can't get anywhere with anyone, then you have no choice but to visit the department/division chair. Bring every assignment with you and any supporting documents (think assignment description, rubrics, etc.). The department/division chair will likely ask if you've looked at or requested those documents.

Say:

> I am turning in assignments and getting grades back, but I need feedback on how to improve my work. I have asked the professor, and she says _____, but I'm still unclear. My grade is suffering. I think I'm doing everything that I can (*make sure that you really are*), and I'd appreciate your advice.

Regarding grade timelines, your best practice is to be proactive. If your syllabus doesn't indicate, say:

> *Professor, when can we expect to receive grades/feedback on discussion questions/quizzes/papers, etc.?*

Then you'll know the timeline in which you can (hopefully) expect this information.

If you haven't received your grade or have no idea where your grade stands because your professor isn't posting the information anywhere (and make sure you check thoroughly first!), say:

> Professor, it has been two weeks (a month, whatever) since we submitted our draft papers, and we have not received feedback or a grade. The final paper is coming up in a week, and I'm concerned we won't have time to implement your suggestions. When should we expect those grades, and can you reconsider the next deadline?

or

Professor, I notice that our grades aren't posted in the course management system. I have no idea where my grade stands, and my progress is important to me. Can I make an appointment with you to go through my grades and find out my overall GPA in the class?

Not That:

Why did you give me this grade?

Be professional rather than oppositional.

The End Note

Cultivate the habit in college of showing that you are someone who wants substantive feedback and that you're someone who will use it. Lots of feedback, even if it feels harsh or overwhelming (not that you should accept mean comments, but rather if you feel frustrated because of a lot of suggested revision) is a *good* thing. Carnegie Mellon professor and author of *The Last Lecture*, Randy Pausch, has one of my favorite quotes about feedback: "When you're screwing up and nobody says anything to you anymore, that means they've given up on you."

If a professor thinks you won't accept or use feedback, you may fail a class. In the workplace, if you can't ask for or use feedback, you might not keep your job or become promoted. For example, one of your most common tasks at work might be to pass documents/reports/projects, etc., back and forth for review. If you don't have a handle on feedback, there could be serious professional ramifications for you.

Request concrete, honest feedback in college. Then, when the working "you" faces performance evaluation time, you'll be ready to ask for clarification and then act on the tips to make yourself even more excellent!

The Career Note

In the workplace, you may receive unclear feedback on a project or a performance review. I wondered how asking for grade clarification in college could help a student learn how to self-advocate in these situations. I asked an international speaker and author of *The Compassionate Geek* for his thoughts:

> To me today, it's unconscionable that a professor or a supervisor would not provide feedback on how a grade or score was determined and specific steps for improvement. In college, the student is paying for instruction. A professor who withholds feedback is simply not doing his or her job. The student should make several attempts using civilized, polite requests to get feedback from the professor and then, if it's still not provided, do everything possible to achieve a desired grade, and, at the conclusion of the semester, report the professor to the department chair. In the case of a boss not providing explanation of scores, that suggests to me an incompetent manager. In the same way that a student should make several civilized and polite requests of the professor, the employee should ask the supervisor for feedback. If it's not forthcoming, it's probably time to find a new job.
>
> Don, customer service/information technology

30. When a Class is Too Easy

What You Might Think:

I can't believe I'm going to spend an entire term in this class. It's so easy! I should have tested out!

What Your Professor Needs to Think (But Probably Doesn't):

I am teaching this course in the only way I know how. I should find out if the rigor is appropriate for the students and for my department.

The Real Story

Nalani was a straight-A student. She took a summer class that was even easier than a no-brainer. Of course, Nalani could have been thrilled. Taking an easy class can be a refreshing brain break from those superhard classes, which are more common.

But this was summer. Nalani didn't want to be wasting her time sitting in a hot classroom not even learning anything. She was even more annoyed that her professor didn't seem to care. In fact, she thought she heard him say that he was "dumbing things down." It was clear he didn't want to be there, either.

"Why am I spending my money on this?" she wondered, not wanting to go back for one more day.

The Backstory

There are times when you might seek out an easy class or finding yourself in one is a relief. But if you feel like Nalani, a high grade in a crappy, simple class may seem like a weak, painful payoff for lost hours of other things you'd rather be doing or classes where you could have really gotten something.

There are many reasons why a class may be too easy:

- You might have previous experience with the subject. Self-explanatory, right?

- You are particularly good at the subject matter. Think strong with math or proven writing ability.

- The professor is purposely creating an easy class so she has less grading to do.

- The professor is inexperienced.

- The professor doesn't have departmental standards or is choosing not to follow them.

- The professor was asked to teach the class at the last minute.

I'm not saying that any of the reasons that have to do with your professor are valid ones, but I at least want you to see why this situation happens. You may find many classes boring, but if you are stuck with a class that is boring and too simplistic for you, there are things you can do.

First, ask for more challenge. Your professor should have instructor's manuals to draw from for quick additional work. You might be able to replace existing assignments with higher-level ones.

Next, see if you can help the professor! Turn that easy class into workplace experience for yourself. Your professor might truly welcome the assistance, as well as some of your confused classmates.

You may also want to find opportunities to learn outside of your classroom. I actually heard about a student whose professor told them that if the course was too easy, they didn't have to show up. Shocking, I know!

Tell your professor you'd rather be in class and what might be helpful to raise the learning capital (if you have ideas). You can also offer to go on your own field trip and write a paper (this would be instead of another assignment). For instance, if you're studying art history, maybe you could spend replacement hours at a local museum. Also mention if something at your job might fit what you are learning in the classroom. For instance, if you're taking a public speaking class and you do regular speaking at your job, see if you can use some of those presentations for your assignments, or ask if you can record yourself in front of your workplace audience.

You may also consider finding other opportunities on campus to supplement your learning in class. Using the public speaking course example again, perhaps there is a communication or speaking club on campus. Or maybe you can find some work study opportunities in the department itself or at a related tutoring center. A few years back, I had a student who took several of my courses during the academic year and then landed paid hours in the college's writing center. Score a similar gig, and your time will feel far more worthwhile.

Likewise, there are bunches of grant-funded positions on campus that allow you to access the hidden college-job market. Again, this could supplement the learning you aren't receiving in that easy class. Inquire at your student union or go to individual services/departments.

Finally, try to stay present in class. Just because the class isn't challenging for you, it doesn't mean that the people in the class aren't interesting. Resist burying yourself in your phone, texting, tweeting or social media-ing to plot after-class fun or to complain about your experience. You never know who you will meet in your classes, so do some networking with others who are there. If your professor isn't challenging you, the least she can do is offer possibilities for collaboration. Ask for group work or some other type of activity if it isn't already being offered.

Ask Yourself This:

There may be times, at school and later at work, when I feel challenged. There may be times that I don't. Am I willing to step up and find ways to challenge myself if necessary?

Think This:

This may not be the ideal class for me because it's easy, but that doesn't mean I can't make something of it. I can seek out ways to challenge myself or, if I

*have a difficult mixture of other classes, I'll feel relief
that I have a break in this one.*

Not That:

*This professor has no business teaching. She doesn't
seem to care about this class.*

You may be right. The professor may have no business teaching. She may not care about the class. I'd love to tell you that every professor loves teaching and wants you to learn, but that would not be the truth. Like in any profession, there are people who are passionate about what they do, people who could take it or leave it, and people who are so burned out that they don't know what to do with themselves (but they can't leave). If you encounter one of the apathetic professors, the worst thing you can do is allow your frustration and anger to alter your work ethic or attitude and potentially risk your grade in what should be a class you could ace. Rise above it.

Say This:

If you want more work:

I'm getting through the assignments and tests with no trouble and scoring As *(your professor's gradebook will bear proof of this, of course)*. Do you have some additional ways I could challenge myself?

If you want to be a teaching assistant:

I'm breezing my way through this class. Maybe I can be of help to you or work with students who are struggling.

If you want to do work outside of the classroom:

I am doing something at work/in an organization that might fit what we're studying. May I replace an assignment?

The End Note

If you land in an easy class, my best advice is to be selfish about it. Keep a positive attitude and show your eagerness for learning, even if the learning isn't being offered to you in an ideal way. Your high work ethic could score you work experience and an extra recommendation letter or two. Then that easy class could turn into one of the most relevant experiences of your college career.

The Career Note

I asked my interviewee what suggestion she would give to someone who feels unchallenged at work. I wondered how self-advocating for a class that is too easy could prepare a student to ask for more responsibility in the workplace.

A suggestion I would give to someone who is feeling unchallenged at work is to communicate with your manager or supervisor. That is the sure way they know they can give you more responsibility or the opportunity for more responsibility. More responsibility or special projects can help relieve boredom and give you more challenge in your job. Self-advocacy is an important skill to hone for all life situations, especially as a student. If you know how to be your own self-advocate, you will always be

able to identify your needs and make requests. In the workplace, knowing how to stand up for yourself and advocate for yourself will show your manager that you are self-assured and confident in who you are and what you need to be successful.

Elouise, disability services

31. Challenging a Professor

What You Might Think:

My dad talks history all the time. I'm pretty sure the dates of that war are incorrect.

or

My paper has an 85, but in the grading system, it's 82.

What You Have the Right to Say:

Can we double-check this? I learned that information a little differently.

and

There seems to be an error in my grade.

The Real Story

In my Interpersonal Communication course a number of years ago, the students and I discussed marriage, based on Knapp's stages of relationship development—the challenging stages, such as differentiation, stagnation, and avoidance. I shared that I had been married briefly at age twenty. Then my father unexpectedly died three months later, and I ended up not staying married (as of this writing, I have been married for twenty years—to a different person).

I am usually pretty candid during the Knapp's discussion without being uncomfortably personal. I am always honest about my own experience with those "downward" stages—like when my husband was laid off, when we struggled with our children, etc. I always qualify that my experiences are just that—my experiences and my opinions. I also state that I believe people become disillusioned when they experience feelings rarely addressed in the context of marriage: ambivalence, frustration, doubt. Many students nodded in agreement (likely thinking of divorce in their own families), or they shared similar insights.

In this particular class, I had an amazing nontraditional student, Ron, who was in his midfifties. As the younger members of the class shared their perceptions about marriage, Ron piped up (in a friendly way): "We're painting marriage in a negative light. I have been married for a long time. This is my second marriage, and I love being with my wife. Being with her energizes me, and she's the first person I want to talk to when we're apart."

I was fine with Ron expressing his thoughts, even though they seemed counter to the discussion that I started and that the class was continuing. Ron built on his own perceptions of Knapp's downward stages, and he did it in a positive way.

This is just one example of challenging a professor, and a mild one at that. Challenging a professor may come in another form: asking a professor to correct or clarify a grade error. You may feel concerned about making this request, but if you receive a grade that has one number or letter, and then you look in your CMS gradebook and find something different, you have the right to correct the error.

The Backstory

Let's start with professors who may share facts with which you disagree or, likewise, their opinions. About those facts: professors learn their material in the following ways:

- Our studies/research in school (e.g., bachelor's, master's, PhD programs)

- What we learn from our mentors in college/real world

- Experts in our field through academic and professional organizations

- Others who teach in our field

- Textbooks, instructor's manuals, etc.

- Popular culture/current events

- Our own experiences

- (There are other ways, too, but you get the picture)

Professors typically present multiple perspectives to you (e.g., your textbook, articles, videos, etc.) We provide the "cognitive" (think brain-based) material to offer knowledge about the subject; this is consistent with those course objectives I discussed in earlier chapters. The objectives are often set by the college, the department, or the professor. Most professors, however, can choose *how* they teach you the base information associated with those objectives.

The hard facts will come from "hard" sources—the text and other materials. But outside of that, your professor will likely have her own interpretations and opinions. You'll have your opinions, too, which may differ from your professor's. At other times, your professor may just plain get a fact wrong, and you know it's wrong. That's all okay. You have the right to respectfully disagree and share your point of view.

You may not have ever been encouraged to disagree with your teachers. But you are in college now. You and your professors are both adults. Sometimes adults disagree.

In effective disagreement, you acknowledge the other person's point of view, then respectfully assert yours: "Professor, I hear what you're saying about _____, but I'd like to share a different perspective." Be calm, be assertive, then listen to the response. Ultimately, you may agree, agree to disagree, or find a space of compromise. Your ideas may spawn intriguing dialogue from the whole class, which is what most professors hope for (as long as the discussion stays respectful).

If your professor responds with sourness just because you have an opposing view, take this in stride. Some professors have high egos, low tolerance for embarrassment, and thrive on their authority. Don't let this deter you from sharing your thoughts. If your professor is truly wrong or you feel differently about the information, then discuss it.

As mentioned, grade disparity is another version of this issue: you were given one grade in one medium (paper, e-mail, etc.), and then your CMS says something different. You might be afraid to confront your professor, particularly if, say, one grade is 85 and the other is 80. Your professor may say the lower grade is actually correct (which might be what your work earned). Or your professor may not acknowledge the error at all (a rare occurrence). The best scenario is if the professor gives you the higher grade based on his error, but that depends on why you received each grade to begin with. You have the right to question this. Your GPA might depend on it.

Likewise, if you submitted an assignment without a grade, you need to address this with your professor right away. I've already talked about how a zero can impact your GPA. You should have some proof that you submitted the assignment (your CMS), but if you had a technology fail, you may not. In fact, you may not even know that your assignment didn't go through.

Always check your CMS to ensure that your dropbox submission made it safely. If you receive any error, e-mail the professor immediately (even if it is right at the deadline time) so she has a record that you attempted to turn it in. Take a screenshot of the error, if possible. Although not ideal, you can attach the assignment to show its completion

A grade discrepancy is usually a simple error. Hopefully your professor will take the inquiry in stride. If she becomes annoyed, just stay businesslike—you need to have proper records of your grades.

Ask Yourself This:

Do I think it is wrong to challenge a prof? What am I afraid will happen if I do? Do I have a general fear about saying what I think to adults? Why do I feel this way?

Think This:

As long as I'm not nasty, I am entitled to disagree and express my opinion. I am also entitled to make sure that my grades are correctly recorded.

Not That:

I don't have a right to speak my mind. I'm just a student.

or

If I see an issue with the accuracy of my grade, my professor will figure it out. It won't be a big deal.

College is supposed to be a safe place to assert your point of view. What's the worst that will happen if your professor disagrees? She won't bite your leg, and he can't give you a bad grade because he doesn't like what you have to say. We all need practice with appropriate conflict management. It's a confidence booster and important experience.

Say This:

The paraphrasing technique can work beautifully when you disagree with someone. Caution: *how* you say what you're saying (your tone, volume, angry face, folded arms, etc.) can impact your listener up to 90 percent more than what you are actually saying, so watch your nonverbal communication:

Professor, I hear you saying _____
(repeat what you recall the professor said in your

own words). I seem to remember the information as
_____.

or

I appreciate what you're saying about _____. I see this differently.

Disclaimer: if you disagree with something *not* class related, don't publicly challenge your professor! Contact her privately.

And if you have an incorrect grade, say:

> I received an 85 on this paper, but an 82 was logged in the online gradebook. Can you explain which is the correct grade?

Disclaimer: if the lower grade Is, indeed, correct, make sure you are told why there was a difference.

or

> I submitted my assignment, but the CMS shows that I have a zero. Perhaps this wasn't received. I had no problems on my end, and the CMS shows my submission at 10:30 p.m.

Disclaimer: make sure the CMS has a record of the submission. Never just hit "attach" and walk away. Confirm successful receipt! If not, take other steps: e-mail your professor right when you see that there is a problem so you have that record.

Not That:

You're wrong!

The word "you" (unless you're saying, "You are so wonderful!") automatically puts the other person on the defensive. Stick to "I" language.

or

You have my grade wrong!

This might be true, but again, show your documentation and use those "I's"!

The End Note

My last tips for encouragement: first, if you challenge anyone, make sure your facts are straight!

Next, if the conversation heats up, stay calm. The first person who raises a voice loses control, as opposed to the person who remains relaxed.

Finally, if you find yourself in a deadlock with your professor, take a breather. Ask for a "part two" to finish the conversation. If you have a genuine grade disagreement, the upcoming chapters will teach you how to handle it.

Bottom line? Don't silence yourself. Sure, you're supposed to learn from your professor, but sometimes, your professor may need to learn from you.

The Career Note

My question involved how self-advocating a genuinely difficult (and possibly unfair) situation prepares students to stand up for themselves at work. I wondered what an industry professional would recommend for students who fear confrontation or don't feel that they deserve to challenge anyone. What if that same student was an employee who was unwilling to challenge a justifiable situation? How would that person be perceived?

It is all about how you challenge: my first manager advised me to never back anyone in a corner because, if you do, their only alternative is to claw their way out. I took that advice to heart, and I don't put others on the defensive. I let folks know that I challenge them because I don't want them to fail. I hope my employees will challenge me if I have the potential to fail.

For example, perhaps you see an error in a math problem your professor is showing the class. If you let him proceed, everyone might learn incorrectly. A polite way to tell a professor is, "Excuse me, I see you wrote this, but I think you meant to do it that way."

A good professor will thank you for both paying attention and for not letting them continue down the wrong path. When people feel you have their best interest at heart, your challenge won't be received in a negative manner.

Employees who are unwilling to self-advocate are viewed as weak and can be taken advantage of very easily, leaving them frustrated. It is important

that folks learn to self-advocate, but in a professional and objective manner. I had one employee who was trying to obtain budget from our customer and, in doing so, he had to present his estimate on the test effort. The manager was very abrasive and told him he didn't believe his estimates. The employee didn't know what to do, as he couldn't find a way to convince this manager that his estimate was correct. He was very upset, afraid to self-advocate, and afraid to present again.

After talking to him, I realized he didn't include the facts and data to support his estimate in the presentation to this manager. I tell my folks no one can argue with facts and data! The next time he had to present, he had all his information and was able to articulate exactly how he built his estimate. The manager approved his budget request right away. It was a real learning lesson for him! Employees who can self-advocate feel empowered, which, in turn, leads to success in the workplace.

Judy, aerospace

32. Handling Grade Issues/ Disputes, Part 1

What You May Think:

This grade/policy change doesn't seem right/fair.

What You Have the Right to Say:

I have a problem with this grade issue/policy change. I would like to understand more and resolve it.

The Real Story

Here are adaptations of e-mails that I've received from students all over the country:

"My professor changed the grading structure partway through the term and never told the class. It was a 10 percent change. Is that allowed?"

"I suspect my professor of discrimination. I am one point away from a C. A D is considered failing."

"I'm failing a class. I e-mailed my instructor about taking an incomplete, but I haven't received a response."

"My professor changed the syllabus after the class was over. He changed the final project percentage because the class grades were too high. This dropped me from a C to a D+, which is failing."

"I have anxiety and depression. I haven't passed a test, and I don't know if I should tell my professor."

"I am in a class that isn't English. Halfway through the semester, the instructor sent an e-mail saying that we'll lose points for grammar or spelling errors. Can the instructor do this, even though it isn't a writing class and the syllabus doesn't say anything about grammar?"

"I'm in a class that includes a group project. We have one final individual assignment, according to the syllabus. I just found out that the instructor is letting the group with the highest grade do the individual assignment as a group. This seems unfair. The professor appears to be playing favorites."

"I am paying $60k yearly in tuition. All the professors in my program use grade curves. I have an 82 percent, based on the curve, which could hold me back in the curriculum and cost me an additional $60k in tuition for another year. I hear that my professor 'seems to enjoy failing students.'"

"My professor decided to add an online proficiency test midterm, in addition to an oral exam. I already signed a syllabus memorandum of understanding which said nothing about this new test. That online test may tank my grade!"

I could fill an entire book with e-mails like these. If you have your own grade/policy Issue right now, clearly You. Are. Not. Alone. (!)

The Back Story

Clearly, grade issues are often complicated. If you find yourself in a legitimately confusing or unfair grade situation, remember that *your basic rights as a student are to know how and why you are being graded and to be treated fairly.*

In this spirit, your professor should not make a grade or policy change that negatively impacts students. I have long relied on this article from Hampton University, written by their legal counsel, on constructing a "legally sound" syllabus: http://provost.hamptonu.edu/cte/legally_sound_syllabi.cfm. In short, the article states that syllabus changes should be created in fairness to the students.

If you witness an unfair grade/policy situation, here are the next steps: first, schedule a meeting with your professor. It won't be easy, but put angry feelings aside. I've said this before: frustration won't solve your problem. Wait until you can discuss the matter assertively and calmly.

Bring all documentation to your meeting: the syllabus, the test (if applicable), the assignment details and what you submitted, e-mails showing that you asked questions—even any class notes related to the situation. Include paperwork that supports your case (Reason #1 why you should never throw away assignments, tests, or assignment descriptions in case you have a problem). A paper trail provides evidence to substantiate your claim. Believe me, your professor will have documentation. Paperwork, either physical or via e-mail/CMS, is our life!

Start the meeting by telling your professor that you are concerned about a grade/policy change. I'll give you exact words in the "Say This" section, but the key is to be professional, specific, and direct. Act inquisitive rather than accusatory. Listen closely. Ask follow-up questions.

If you resolve the issue, awesome! You're hopefully all good and can celebrate your ability to successfully confront conflict. But if the issue remains, it's time to research the official college policy on resolving a grade dispute.

Every college has an official dispute/grievance policy, located on the college website or in the student handbook. The student senate, the registrar, Educational Planning/Advising, and even Counseling Services can help you locate and interpret the policy. You will likely deal with college personnel aside from your professor, so become well versed in the procedure.

An official grade dispute usually requires documentation. You may have to fill out an official form and add evidence (the documents you used with your professor). Write a clear description of the problem and its ramifications. This goes without saying, but no blame or venom; use that "I" language. Other people will likely read your words; inappropriateness will cloud the issue.

The college policy may require you to go to the next person in command *before* submitting the paperwork. That's fine: resolving the problem at the department or division level may be quicker. An official dispute often requires a committee review, and committees may not hold regular meetings. You could be in academic and financial limbo, which you don't want.

Some students worry about the impact of a grade dispute on their "permanent record." True, the college likely keeps official documentation in your file, but the records are confidential and can't negatively impact your entry into another college or a job.

My next piece of advice is to argue the proper charge. You may have to "categorize" your dispute. It's pretty hard to prove malicious intent ("she likes failing students") or even discrimination—even if you are certain of it. The burden of proof would be on you to show a trail of evidence (e-mails, testimony from other students, etc.), and still, this would be subjective. Stick with hard data about your grade, the details of the assignment/exam, and the original syllabus policies. Those are more provable and debatable.

My last tip: mind the big picture and be realistic. If you aren't leaving the college, you could encounter the dean, VP, or professor again. In fact, many administrators teach intermittently—a huge reason to be professional. Relationships can change in a heartbeat, and that professor you can't stand today could be a mentor tomorrow. For real!

Also, you aren't likely to get the professor fired, unless that person is part-time faculty, and even then, it's not so easy. A professor may be reprimanded for the issue but not let go. You may feel that this person shouldn't be teaching, but you can't fix that. Focus on resolving your problem rather than a larger punishment for the professor.

Ask Yourself This:

Am I afraid to dispute a grade or policy that I feel is unfair? What am I afraid will happen? How would I feel if I stand up for myself and I am successful?

Think This:

If I genuinely believe that I have been wronged by a grade or policy change, I have the right to seek resolution.

Not That:

I can't "win" against a professor. They aren't going to change anything.

If you don't speak up, you have no chance to resolve your issue. You have to try.

or

My professor will retaliate if I question her.

Your professor can't take revenge on you for inquiring about a grade/policy problem. If she does, you'll have more of a basis for your complaint.

or

No one will believe me.

They will if you have proper documentation and a legitimate issue! Also, make sure you didn't drop the ball somewhere before pointing the finger.

Say This:

> Professor, I would like to meet with you regarding a grade/policy issue. I received X grade, and I am concerned about it. I'd like you to explain how you arrived at my grade. Here is the information that made me think my grade would be _____ (*show your documentation*).
>
> You can add, "This has a negative impact on me because _____."

or

> Professor, the syllabus states _____, and I understand that you would like to make a change to _____. This will have a negative outcome for me (*explain specifically or show your documentation*), and I would like you to reconsider.

I am really pissed that I got a _____.

or

That change is totally unfair!

All may be true, but if your professor feels attacked, she won't listen to your rationale. And you'll sound unprofessional and irrational.

The End Note

You may wonder what advice I gave to each student in the earlier situations. I'll summarize:

Changing standards partway through the term or at the end: not allowed if it causes great harm to the students, but happens all the time. The professor should lay out the reason for the proposed change and consult the class or receive consultation from her department/division chair. Either way, transparency is key; the impact should be explained.

Discrimination/professor "enjoys" failing students: unless many students report concerns, difficult to prove. A formal grievance could be filed, but this would likely not change the grade. Instead, focus on discrepancies between the assignment and the final grade, quality of the work, etc.

Asking about an incomplete: professors can use their discretion for an incomplete, but not generally for academic reasons (e.g., you were doing poorly and needed more time). Instead, an incomplete could be used for a sudden life emergency (medical, family member death, etc.). An incomplete does not negatively impact your transcript, and you don't pay for the class again. Instead, you and your professor draw up an official contract to complete the work in a set amount of time. If you don't complete the work, your grade reverts to what it would have been. One note about an incomplete is that it can be helpful while working out a grade dispute, so you can always ask.

Anxiety/depression or any other emotional/physical issue: talk to the professor, but even more importantly, if you have official documentation, go to your Disability Services department for official advocacy and accommodations. Your professor likely won't change your grades based on a medical situation, but Disability Services can help you be proactive in getting more time, assistance, etc. Counseling services is also a must for this and any situation that is hindering your grade success (no official documentation needed).

Abruptly altering assignment parameters: if the professor suddenly sees a problem, it is reasonable to change the scope of an assignment/exam. The change should also be reasonable: for instance, revising grading structure to "force" students into better grammar/spelling/punctuation isn't unheard of if there are sudden issues. This wouldn't have to be an actual policy change unless grammar, etc. was not graded at all and then suddenly it's worth 50 percent of the grade.

Group/individual assignments: a professor should not do for one (individual or group) what she isn't doing for the class. A transparent conversation should happen if there is a significant change, and even then, students should be permitted to voice concerns.

Change to the syllabus after student sign-off: again, changes should never occur to hinder student success. If a test is added, then this should be clearly explained to the students and the grade weight consistent with the rest of the syllabus (or in replacement of another assignment/exam). A sudden exam that could tank a student's entire grade should never happen. Also, technically, if a student is required to sign off and "agree" to syllabus standards, then changes should also be agreed upon in writing—with sign-off.

There is another way to look at this situation: many syllabi include the word "tentative." Your professors can add assignments and assessments, as necessary, to respond to student needs. Sometimes, professors can't predict this until gauging the needs of their students. However, the alteration should not single-handedly dismantle your grade.

One last word of encouragement: never risk destroying your education or reputation over a grade dispute. You are not the underdog. If you communicate professionally and rationally, you have every chance for a positive outcome, and you'll maintain others' respect while you're asserting yourself. Even if you aren't successful, stand up for yourself. You have the right to be fully informed.

33. Handling Grade Issues/ Disputes, Part 2

I can't work things out with this professor, and I don't know what to do.

Who is your department/division chair? I feel that I need an outside perspective on this situation.

The Real Story

I was days away from delivering my youngest son (who, as of this writing, is eight), and so incredibly ready for maternity leave.

My phone rang; it was my division chair: "A student made a complaint."

Ugh. I have had so few student disputes in all of my years, but they are upsetting nonetheless. My division chair said that I was accused of being unfair because the student earned a C on an outline. The student never addressed the issue with me but fast-tracked to my chair. I'll share the outcome of this situation later in this chapter.

Here's another version of a student complaint about another professor, adapted from an e-mail:

> "My classmates and I have a professor who behaves unprofessionally, discusses participating in inappropriate activities, and mentions other professors and students anonymously, but we can figure it out. My classmates and I feel this behavior is unprofessional and unacceptable. What should we do?"

Sometimes, students feel they need a larger voice on their side. The key is knowing when going higher is appropriate and how to start that process.

The Backstory

Let me explain how each of these scenarios would play out. First, the student angry with me over the grade:

Step 1: The department/division chair would ask the student if they spoke with me and, if not, would recommend they do so.

Step 2: If the student did talk to me but couldn't resolve the situation, then Student should bring documentation/proof (your graded paper, syllabus, copy of the assignment—anything that can support your position) to the department/division chair. The chair would review documents before making recommendations.

Quick side note: if the student refused to come to me, the chair might offer up a three-way meeting so the student felt they had an ally, or the chair may privately ask to hear my side.

Step 3: The chair would a) make recommendations to the student that don't involve me; b) set up a meeting between the three of us (the chair facilitates); or c) make recommendations to me and ask me to follow up with the student (or the chair would follow up).

The issue would then hopefully resolve to your satisfaction. In the "End Note," I'll describe what to do if that doesn't happen.

Now scenario #2: the badly behaving professor. Students feel powerless in these circumstances because they can't confront the professor. If you remain silent, your learning will likely be impacted by general uneasiness. Also, someone should know about the professor's actions. Here is what to do:

Step 1: Meet with the department/division chair rather than the professor. A third party makes sense with a "behavioral" rather than "procedural" problem.

(Side note: other classmates should do the same thing. Single voices make a stronger argument, rather than a representative).

Step 2: I'll focus on process here, but find the tips in the "Say This" section below: the department/division chair would confront the issue with the professor on your behalf (anonymously, of course). If the chair suggests you see the professor (unlikely), ask if they can be present.

Step 3: Request a follow-up meeting with the chair so the matter doesn't fade away. They probably won't provide specifics of their discussion, but hopefully will offer some reassurance. Say, "How should I follow up with you about this situation?"

Step 4: If the chair does not respond to your concerns satisfactorily, tell your school's counseling services office, an academic dean, a student affairs/student services officer, or your advisor what is going on. They would investigate the situation. Of course, they'll probably ask if you tried to speak with the department/division chair. Let's hope your situation wouldn't come to that, though.

You may worry that your professor will find out you "told on them." They wouldn't. College staff are bound by confidentiality. Don't feel guilty about making a case for a comfortable classroom environment. If your professor is behaving unprofessionally, that needs to be investigated by a college official. Your class, grades, and mental state should not suffer.

Ask Yourself This:

Do I feel afraid to speak to someone higher up about problems with my professor? Am I afraid I won't be taken seriously or that I will suffer in some way?

Think This:

If I am dealing with an unfair or inappropriate situation, I have the right to seek assistance from someone other than my professor.

Not That:

I won't be taken seriously.

As long as you follow proper hierarchy, you will be taken seriously. If you are off base, the chair, or whomever else you're talking to, will let you know.

or

I will get in trouble if I go above my professor's head.

As long as you are honest and have information to back you up, you won't. For the record, even students who spew fury only suffer a strained reputation, unless they breach the Student Code of Conduct.

or

The problem will go away.

Probably not. Trust your gut and stand up for yourself.

Say This:

If you can't resolve the issue with your professor, say:

> I appreciate your taking the time to meet with me, but I would like to discuss this matter with a division/ department chair for a second opinion.

When you meet with the chair, say:

> I've met with Professor _____, and we couldn't resolve the issue. As you can see, the syllabus states that we will be graded on _____. The comments on my paper do not show that _____ was taken into consideration. I have a copy of my other grades in this class and also a previous paper which had a higher grade. The requirements don't seem to match the way I was graded. I'd like your advice.

In the second situation, say to the chair, "I am concerned about my experience in Professor Jones' class this semester. I have not spoken with Professor Jones directly because of the nature of these concerns. I could use some advice about how to discuss these issues, and I'm hoping you can help."

Then give concrete examples:

> I have three issues that have become a pattern this semester. First, the professor makes continued references to inappropriate outside activity. Second, the professor is publicly disclosing issues with other students and professors. Although anonymous, we can figure out who he is talking about. Finally, the professor lashes out at our class.

Disclaimer #1: In the situation about the grade dispute, if the professor can justify how the grade was earned, the chair will not recommend an override unless there is a major discrepancy. Case in point: I showed my division chair the criteria that led to my student's C. I had even given early advice that the student didn't use.

Disclaimer #2: In the situation about the professor's behavior, these issues do not resolve immediately. If the professor has tenure, they can't be fired without thorough process. The solution may take time, but the chair can help you figure out how to get through the class (or they will take action with the professor).

Not That:

> I want to get my professor in trouble, so I'll go to her boss!

It takes a lot for faculty to "get in trouble" on a college campus.

or

> If you don't take care of this problem, I'm going to go straight to the college president (or dean, or board of trustees)!

Threats won't get you very far, particularly since the college president (or whoever) will go back down the ladder to dissect the problem. Administrators *do* care. That isn't the issue. But out of fairness, they will have to investigate the problem and will likely ask the department/division chair, "Do you know anything about this?" Then they will likely let that person handle the problem, or at least bring them in. The administrator doesn't want to breach the chain of command either!

Remember: you may embarrass yourself by going higher up the chain of command than is appropriate, and your actual problem will have less of a chance for resolution.

If you can't resolve the issue with a department/division chair, then find a dean who oversees your professor's area (academic, professional-technical, transfer, etc.). An academic advisor, counselor, or a student activities officer (an employee of the college) can also advise about the next point of contact.

The End Note

You have numerous resources if you are struggling with a professor, even aside from the chair. If you have a documented disability, contact the Disability Services office, which can advocate on your behalf. Also, college counseling centers help you deal with any academic or nonacademic issue getting in the way of your education. Those services are typically free or very low cost. You also have your advisor and tutoring centers. Students in tutoring centers may know your professor's expectations and can help you identify why you're receiving a particular grade/feedback.

Also realize that if you reach an impasse with your professor, he may recommend bringing in a third party (the chair). I've definitely said from time to time: "I think we've reached a point where I would like to bring my division chair in on this conversation."

Standing up for yourself over a legitimate issue is critical practice for your self-advocacy skills. Doing so can feel horribly uncomfortable and nauseatingly intimidating, but you are an adult, and you have rights to a comfortable classroom climate and to have a professional classroom leader.

There may be a time in your professional future or even in another type of situation (like a customer service problem) when you will go over someone's head for advice. You'll be ready to follow the proper channels and use the right words.

The Career Note

This is an extension of the discussion in Chapter 31. When we're talking about self-advocacy or disagreements between students and professors, what we're really talking about is conflict management and self-advocacy. Cultivating both skills is critical for any job. I asked, "Have you had an experience where an employee disagreed with you in a negative way? How could that employee have used a more positive approach? What encouragement would you give a student on practicing these skills in a relatively 'safe' environment such as college?"

I had an employee who rolled her eyes and sighed every time she disagreed with something I said in a meeting. It was distracting, disrespectful, and, in the end, made both of us look bad. She put me in a position where, in meetings, everyone watched to see how I would handle her actions. It was very stressful for myself and other attendees. Nothing I said about changing her behavior reached her.

Finally, I learned that she was a very successful poker player. She loved to tell stories about her success in that arena. One day, I asked (privately), "How is it that when you play poker, no one knows you have four aces, but in my meeting, everyone knows that you vehemently disagree with what I or other folks discuss in the meeting?"

I explained that if she disagreed in a positive light, that would make the tone of the meeting much more positive and productive. Others would be willing to listen to her point of view, which was often right!

She realized that her body language and expressions were toxic and disruptive. She worked very hard to change her demeanor, and she started disagreeing in a productive manner. Then people listened to her! Whenever I would see her smiling, walking out of meetings, all I could think of was, "four aces." As a manager, I was so glad to help this employee grow professionally.

It is important to learn these skills before even entering the workplace. When talking to a professor, no good can come from being disrespectful. It will only put the professor on the defensive and will dilute your argument. If, instead, you are respectful, *present your facts, and make a connection, you will find they will at least listen to your point of view, and you'll establish a positive relationship going forward. You might need a letter of recommendation someday, and that very same professor might be so impressed with the way you disagreed.*

Judy, aerospace

34. Teaching Style/ Dealing with a Boring Class

What You Might Think:

I'd rather put a staple through my finger than listen to this professor's monotone voice one more second.

What You Have the Right to Say:

I'm struggling with the format of this class.

The Real Story

Picture this: a 115-degree summer day in Las Vegas. A white-haired professor with a tweed sport coat (on a 115-degree summer day?) who lectured from a yellow legal pad for Three. Long. Hours. twice a week in an environmental science class. Then picture me: sweaty from just walking across the parking lot, wondering how I will make it through one more lecture without losing my mind. It was only the second week of class with six long weeks to go!

I started with a good attitude, and oh, did I try *hard* to stay attentive. On the first day of class, I diligently took notes. On the second day, I took some notes and doodled on the side of my page. Lightning bolts and flowers. Day three, more doodling, less note taking. Day four, I wasn't taking notes, I was *passing* notes (there wasn't texting yet) with some other miserable, bored soul. I had given up. Some other students had, too, playing on their Gameboy consoles in the back of the room. Professor Tweed never seemed to notice.

I was furious, and I took the anger out on myself. I hated the material because, in my opinion, there was no motivation on the professor's part to make it interesting. My fury only stood to hurt me: Professor Tweed's class was all multiple-choice tests based on the textbook and those dratted lectures!

I'd love to tell you that I was new to college, a teenager, but I wasn't. I was almost thirty years old. So I had even less patience for this boring instructional style that was as old as the one-room schoolhouse. Maybe Professor Tweed cared at one point in his career, but that wasn't evident with the disinterested crew of students on any of those boiling Las Vegas days.

My only goal was to pass the class, even with a C. I could average that up with As elsewhere. I was graduating with an AA transfer degree, and my incoming bachelor's program wasn't competitive. I just had to keep my GPA between 3.0 and 3.5, though I personally wanted so much more. I was so soured that I never wanted to revisit environmental science again; I made a desperate bargain with myself to get through the class. How sad that my expectations became so low.

I'd love to say that this was a onetime occurrence in my college career. It wasn't. I also experienced:

- An education class that met for six hours on a weekend day, in a dark room lit only by a PowerPoint presentation on a screen. The professor never used the restroom, so we never had a break.

- A biology class that was a full-on lecture with intricate PowerPoint slides and no opportunity for student interaction.

- A math class where the professor mumbled at the whiteboard, rarely making eye contact with the students.

These experiences were right before the year 2000. Not long ago. Can you relate? Do you have horror stories of your own? I bet I know the answer.

The Back Story

There is a huge difference between professors like the ones I mentioned and those who mesmerize you because they clearly love teaching and being with students. A professor doesn't need to be "showy" or entertaining in order to be interesting, relevant, or connected.

Professors teach in different ways largely because they learn to teach in different ways. A shocking truth: many professors don't take a lot of courses on *how* to teach college. They learn through one or two classes in their own graduate program, or they may teach 100- and 200-level courses in their master's or PhD program as part of what is called a graduate assistantship (think paid tuition, research and/or teaching experience, and even small amounts of stipend money). Graduate assistants may have some educator training, but every college differs in how they coach future faculty. We're not talking about the same teaching certificate required of elementary and secondary school teachers. Anyone with a master's degree or PhD in their discipline can teach college—and they can do this without formal "teacher" training.

So if your professor is a thought leader in molecular biology, that person may not know what to do with students staring at him. Hence, many professors simply mimic what they've seen in their own faculty—for better or worse. This means that your professor, who didn't get much training on how to teach college, might have inadvertently taken on his professors' unfavorable styles!

We also can't forget about personality. Some people are dynamic. Others aren't. Some professors believe that they are in the classroom to impart expertise and wisdom and students are there to intake information. Other professors are open, accessible, and interested in creating dialogue with students. These professors believe they are learning just as much *from* their students.

Just because a professor isn't outgoing doesn't mean he doesn't care about student learning. Truly, this person may not know how to do anything other than ramble endlessly like Professor Tweed. However, even when I tried to ask Professor Tweed if he would consider letting students form groups, answer questions—anything—he clammed up. Clearly not comfortable with or open to those ideas.

I asked for a different classroom experience out of courage and desperation. If you are miserable in your class, you have three choices:

1. Live with it.

2. Drop the class.

3. Talk to the professor about changing something.

I can tell you from experience that living with an awful class situation will frustrate you. You'll feel like you are putting in seat time, wasting that portion of your life. However, dropping the class stands to hurt you, too. You could throw off your graduation timeline or have to deal with the professor again because he is the only one who teaches the class.

That leaves one solution: do what I did, and ask for a change. I can't promise that you can alter years of not-great teaching behaviors, but you can certainly try. You owe it to yourself, and your input might help that professor, too.

Ask Yourself This:

What have I done on other occasions when I didn't click with a teacher/professor's teaching style? Still pay attention? Lose the information entirely? How do I function in other situations where I have to sit and listen (meetings, house of worship, work training) and I am not engaged by the situation or the person speaking?

An alternate question, just in case it's more you than the professor:

Do I suffer from a short attention span? Do I believe I should be entertained in order to stay focused? What can I do to help myself? What are one to three things this professor can do differently that might help me?

Think This:

I have a right to be engaged in my education, even though I won't find every professor engaging.

You will love some professors' teaching styles and not others. You can't fault your professor if their personality doesn't click with yours. You can only control your own habits.

Try to reevaluate your interest in the topic, ask more questions in class, offer to trade notes with a classmate (which will force you to pay attention—that person will be counting on you), or bargain with yourself that if you can focus for the hour, you'll reward yourself with an extra hour of something you enjoy later.

Say This:

> I'm struggling with the format of this class. I learn best when I'm _____ (doing something, talking about the information, asking questions, etc.). I know you have a lot to share with us. I appreciate how much information you provide in your lectures, and I want to learn this material. I am wondering if we can try:

(*pick options that you are comfortable suggesting*)

- Group discussion

- Adding a Q & A period after each section

- Asking questions during lectures

- Submitting anonymous questions before class that you answer during class

- Doing activities related to the material

- Assigning a section to students and allowing them to present the information

- *(Or any of your own ideas. Think of a teacher whose style you enjoyed.)*

If your request doesn't work, you'll have to figure out what to do next. Talking to someone higher up probably won't do you much good in the current term. Teaching style isn't a quick fix. And, unless there is a glaring situation impacting numerous students, this could be an individual perception. In the meantime, how do you survive? Here are some strategies:

Record the lectures and listen to them later. I know you don't want to suffer again, but doing so in your own home with a snack may make things more tolerable.

Say to the professor:

Can you share lecture notes or PowerPoint files with us?

Maybe the professor will post the information on a course management system, and then you can make sideline notes without feeling the pressure to listen to every word. You can try to come up with creative ways to remember the material, especially if it will be on an exam.

Ask questions during the lectures. You always have the right to do this, and you never know when it might spark the professor to allow a different type of environment.

Not That:

This professor sucks!

or

This professor is a jerk! She doesn't care that we aren't paying attention!

Do not turn the anger on yourself. Also, many professors who can't engage students already feel it by the deafening silence of their classroom. They may just not know what to do.

The End Note

You may feel scared to talk to your professor about their teaching style. If you just can't do it, remember that you'll probably have a class evaluation. As long as you write professionally (give specific ideas, spell correctly, use proper grammar), you can give suggestions that may be seen by the professor's superior, a tenure/posttenure committee, etc.

What I'm recommending in this chapter is not easy. Even if your professor makes one small change, this can make a big difference in your experience. Hopefully, he will see that you are helping him become better at the art of teaching!

The Career Note

When I think about a student offering suggestions about a professor's teaching style, we're really talking about a version of feedback—just in the other direction. I thought about how a boss might handle feedback, whether solicited or unsolicited. Here's what I learned:

> *In my industry, goals are given, and the team is autonomous in how those goals are achieved. I will meet with them to review strategies to achieve those goals, but each member of my team may have a different approach, which allows them to feel a*

sense of independent accomplishment and pride in their work.

I typically receive a lot of engagement from my team when requesting feedback. I believe the reason for this engagement is that they know that I will take the information and bring the core issues to corporate leadership who can take action on the feedback within the organization.

I think if people feel that feedback is solicited but then they don't see tangible results, then they feel that it's not worth the effort to provide feedback— particularly candid feedback.

However, the team also acknowledges that not all feedback will receive action.

Connie, national health insurance

---

35. Learning About/ Evaluating Your Professors

What You Might Think:

I've heard awful things about Professor Scary. Her scores on Ratemyprofessor.com are terrible.

What You Have the Right to Say (in writing):

(Before class begins)

> Professor Scary, I'd like to ask some questions about the class.

(And as class is ending)

> Here is exactly how Professor Scary impacted me and my learning.

The Real Story

In 2012, my score on *Ratemyprofessor.com* was 4.8 (5.0 scale, eight respondents). Fast forward five years, and my score fell to 4.0 (thirteen respondents). My rating tanked from an online summer course where some students didn't like the requirements.

The drop saddened me. I take tremendous pride in my teaching over fifteen years. I've taught thousands of students; I have thousands of high-scoring student evaluations. *Ratemyprofessor.com* doesn't show this.

Would you avoid my class based on *Ratemyprofessor.com*? If so, you might miss what countless students feel is an awesome experience. Thirteen students' perceptions, good or bad, can't tell the whole story—even if all those reviews were stellar.

Bottom line: you deserve to know about your professor ahead of time—if you want to. You also have the right to evaluate your professor at the end of the term.

The Backstory

Students ask, "Who should I take?" and "Who is easy?" You can look online or talk to another professor or a student. A professor probably won't say negative things about a colleague. A fellow student is chancy; students may have different perspectives. Who will you listen to?

And who's "easy"? Getting "easy" grades may shortchange your experience. My thesis advisor in grad school was deemed the "meanest." All true: my thesis repeatedly bled with edits. But I was the only student in my department to present at an international conference. Hence, I had a wonderful experience!

Trust your gut. "Researching" a professor takes time, so plan for it. You don't want to miss registering for another class in the meantime. Here are your options:

a. Visit the professor during office hours and ask for a syllabus; or,

b. Sit in on a class before you register; or,

c. Ask previous students what *they* thought of the professor (again, risky).

And here are some things you could find out about the professor:

- The overall pace/tone of the class (check the syllabus)

- The professor's teaching style (sit in on a class)

- The prof's approachability/availability/personality (visit the professor in her office. If she seems busy, don't let that deter you.)

- Requires a lot of tests/assigns "busywork" (the syllabus)

A note of caution: you won't love or like every professor. If you can learn and have a decent working relationship, other positives are a bonus. If you handpick all professors, you may be left with few people from whom to take classes.

Every professor will teach you *something about yourself.* You need experience dealing with all types of people, so embrace the opportunity.

Now, on to student evaluations: many students feel evaluations don't matter, but your voice is critical. Every school handles evaluations differently, but here are some generalities:

First, if your professor doesn't have tenure (this person has met the college's requirements for teaching, research, service, etc., and he has a guaranteed job) but is on the tenure track (on the way to tenure), then your professor is probably required to do class evaluations. A tenure committee reviews the evaluations (the group of peers/administrators/staff evaluating his performance).

Perceptions of professor performance varies, depending on the institution. A professor with strong research or interests deemed important to administration could receive subpar teaching evaluations and still receive tenure. If problems repeatedly show up, the professor receives coaching.

After tenure, some colleges don't require regular student evaluations unless the professor is reevaluated (posttenure process) or going for a promotion (which may only happen every few years). You may think, *At other jobs, your performance is evaluated every year—sometimes more!* Yes! This is why some oppose tenure. Sometimes, professors get it and are never reviewed again unless numerous students complain (and maybe not even then).

If your professor is part-time or a lecturer, evaluations usually occur every term or on a more regular schedule. But still, a poorly performing professor might not be let go. Why? Three reasons:

a. full-time faculty already teach maximum class load;

b. the discipline is hard to fill; or

c. the part-timer teaches when others won't: early morning, evenings, or even weekends.

Distribution of evaluations also varies from college to college. Many course evaluations occur in class without the professor present. They may be delivered online, mailed, etc.

Finally, evaluation content varies: many colleges have standard questions, regardless of discipline; others have discipline/department-specific questions.

Something ultracritical: colleges want students to speak freely, without backlash. Therefore, your professor won't see your evaluation until after your grade is submitted and after you've left for the term. Also, handwritten evaluations are often typed by an administrative secretary so they can't be identified.

Evaluate *every* class that you can. Be specific with your compliments and your complaints (nastiness won't be taken seriously). Many professors take students' advice seriously. But be realistic about your performance: if you slacked, that's about you.

If you are not offered an evaluation but want to share your thoughts, ask a department/building secretary to whom you can direct an e-mail.

Ask Yourself This:

How much do I need to know about my professors before I take a class with them? How will I feel if I find out information about the prof that I don't like? What strategies can I use to get through the class? If I stay with this difficult experience, what can I learn from it?

and

Do I know the evaluation process at my college? Do I perceive that my evaluation will be taken seriously?

Do I believe something bad will happen if I nega-
tively evaluate my professor?

Think This:

I can learn about my professor, but I have to be
realistic. Even if I don't care for the professor or hear
that other students didn't like her, I'll find a way to
deal with it. There are many resources to help me if
I'm struggling.

and

I have a right to use my evaluation to say whether
or not I felt that a class—and particularly the profes-
sor—was effective.

Not That:

I can't take this professor! I've heard terrible things!

What if no one else teaches the class? Will you change your
schedule—or worst, your major—to avoid that person? Believe
that you can handle any personality type you come into contact with. Because you can!

or

My professor will see my evaluation and then give
me a bad grade.

No college wants you to be negatively affected by your evaluation. Don't sugarcoat your evaluation to get a good grade.
That won't happen either.

or

There is no evaluation, so I won't get to say what I think.

Find out how you can submit anyway.

or

The professor has tenure. What I say won't get him fired.

This could be true, but someone will get the heads-up that your professor needs to strengthen his teaching.

Say This:

If you want to meet a professor early, e-mail and say,

Professor, I'm considering taking your class next term, and I am wondering if I can stop by and meet you. I'd like to pick up a syllabus. Even one from this term or last would be fine.

Or visit during office hours. Say:

Hello, I'm _____, and I'm going to be in your class next term. I wanted to learn about the class. Do you have a syllabus I can take a look at?

During this meeting, discuss concerns you have:

I have extreme speech anxiety and am scared to take this class.

I have accommodations set up with the disability office. Here is documentation, and I'd like to discuss what I'll need.

I struggle with math. Where I can go for additional help?

If you are presented with a student evaluation, respond with honesty and specificity:

I appreciated how quickly Professor Jones responded to e-mail.

or

I thought the professor was extremely helpful when the class was confused on Chapter 2.

Focus on how effectively your professor managed class and taught the subject matter.
Have constructive criticism? Say:

Our class could have used a different type of review for the midterm. Maybe we could have broken out into small groups and quizzed each other.

If your ideas are reasonable, you have a better chance of being taken seriously. The biggest changes in my teaching derived from students with great recommendations.
Use "I" language for all your comments. Own your words.
If you are not offered a student evaluation, say to your professor:

Will we have an opportunity to evaluate this class?

If the professor says,

> No, I'm not doing evaluations this term,

you can say,

> I'd like to give some feedback. Should I write e-mail that to you?

To remain confidential, ask/e-mail a department/division chair or building secretary,

> I would like to evaluate my class, but the professor is not doing evaluations this term. How can I give feedback?

Ask your fellow classmates to do the same.

Preface your request with a reason:

> I faced a major problem, and I feel someone should know.

> *or*

> This class was amazing, and I wanted to share my good experience.

Not That:

(To another student);

> So, you had Professor Jones last term. How was he?

It's tempting, I know, but put feedback in context: if the student failed, it doesn't mean you will. Likewise, an incredible experience may or may not happen to you, too. Instead, ask,

> Do you have recommendations to help me in this class?

And with respect to evaluations, don't say,

> I hated this class and this professor.

or

> The professor is mean.

Word your comments professionally, or you won't be taken seriously. Then no one will know *why* you hated the class and your professor. Be specific! Say,

> The professor showed up late every week.

or

> The professor doesn't answer student questions.

or

> The professor doesn't return work for weeks.

or

> The professor talks down to students.

or

The professor dresses ugly.

Your professor's personal attributes don't matter unless something concretely impedes your learning:

The professor's heavy cologne triggered migraines.

The End Note

Someday, an interviewer may ask if you've worked with difficult people. Your experience with an unlikeable professor can provide you with a ready answer of how you thrived, so be glad!

And one last thought on *Ratemyprofessor.com*: administrators won't see your thoughts, and neither may your professor. Then there's no chance to fix an issue.

Student evaluations help you practice self-advocacy. You'll probably give constructive feedback to a supervisor or one of your own employees someday. Use this opportunity skillfully. Change *can* come from you and your words!

So say them—er, write them!

The Career Note

I wanted to ask someone in industry if they've experienced a difficult professor who ultimately prepared them for challenging dynamics in the workplace:

> *My favorite professor in graduate school was also the toughest and not my highest grade. On the first day, he indicated that there would be no excuse for not showing up on time or prepared unless we were*

deathly ill. During lectures, he'd simply stop calling on you if you were not bringing your "A game." I've never worked so hard for a B+ in my life. I took every class he offered, including electives. A group of students in a cohort after mine refused to take his first-year class, required for all of us, protesting his toughness. It made me wonder what they would do once out of grad school and in the real world.

Years later, I know I am a better consultant and manager because of his influence. If I had read a review of him and opted for easier classes and a professor with a softer approach, I would have lost out on a true learning experience.

Hazel, management consulting

---

36. When the Whole Class Fails

What You Might Think:

"Ugh. I failed the midterm, and so did the whole class."

What You Have the Right to Say:

"Can we discuss why the whole class failed?"

The Real Story

Ever experience this? The teacher/professor comes into the classroom, pained expression all over her face. She says, "This last test didn't go so well. Most of you failed."

Maybe you felt guilty or even—stupid.

What most students don't realize is that if an entire class fails *anything*—an assignment, an exam, or any other graded/measured product—there is far more to that story.

The Back Story

The suggestions in this chapter may test you more than any failed exam. Before I get to those, let me remind you about course objectives in your syllabus. If what you learn in class is very different from the course objectives, there will be discrepancies in assignment/exam grades. An example: I am not an expert in small group communication. In my college's 101 course (Intro to Communication), our course objectives involve interpersonal communication, small group communication, and public speaking. Years ago, our departmental exam included small group communication questions.

If I minimally cover small group communication, my students may fail those questions. Ever say, "That test didn't cover anything we talked about in class!"? This happens when curriculum doesn't match the end product.

Now the key issue: the whole class failed. But why? (By failing, I mean 60–65 percent or below):

* The entire class didn't study.

Possible, not probable. Students are all over the map with grades; it's hard to fathom that every single student didn't study and, as a result, failed.

* What was taught didn't match what was assigned/assessed.

More likely. Perhaps your professor has current industry experience and teaches you different content than required by the department. If you are tested on the departmental requirements, low test scores will result. And, of course, the example where the professor skimps on a teaching a topic. Potential test failure.

- The test had flaws.

Very likely. There is science behind what makes a "good" and "bad" test question (I took a tests and measurements course). Many professors watch students score low on questions but may not realize the question was problematic to begin with.

Some departments constantly analyze test data. In past years, my department collected test scores, reviewing and changing problem questions. My department also once used a common persuasive rubric. If many students scored low on information literacy, we'd need to focus instruction around incorporating credible sources.

Not all faculty scrutinize assignments/assessments this way. One of my professors, Dr. Clifford McClain, used to say: "If the whole class falls, there's probably something wrong with the instrument or the instruction." Therefore, we faculty should ask ourselves, "How thoroughly did I cover that material? Is there something wrong with the questions or instructions?"

You may be ready to confront every professor/teacher who gave you a failing grade. It's not that simple. This situation only applies if the *majority* of your class does poorly.

And if that happens? Talk to your professor! It's intimidating, I know. You may think, *What right do I have to question?* If you ask inquisitively, with sincerity, not entitlement, your professor will hopefully investigate the problem. I can't promise, but your inquiry could lead to positive changes.

Don't rush to report your professor to a division/department chair. A failed test is not a quick fix, but rather the sign of a larger curricular issue requiring further investigation. Academic freedom exists for a reason. Always start with your professor, then go up the ladder.

Ask Yourself This:

Am I willing to find out what the class average was on a given exam or assignment? What am I afraid my professor will say/do if I ask questions? What positive things could happen?

Think This:

I can tactfully ask my professor if she is willing to discuss a particular assignment/test. I can say that I'm interested to learn how the class is doing as a whole (if I don't already know this), and I am wondering if we can review the test to see if a lot of students had problems with certain questions.

Not That:

My professor could fail me just because I questioned him.

If you remain professional, your professor hopefully won't perceive a personal attack. If your professor is well rooted in his instruction, there is no reason for defensiveness. Sometimes we professors forget that we should be in the business of learning, too.

Say This:

Before you meet with the professor, formulate a crystal-clear goal:

- Retaking the exam

- Grading on a curve

- Having a discussion with the whole class about areas of confusion

- Throwing out certain sections of an exam if a certain number of students failed

- Allowing students to take a different type of exam

- Adding an assignment to help comprehension/application (not extra credit. You know how I feel about that!)

You don't have to ask for any of these things, but they are requests you can make. If you say,

> You should do something about the fact that we all failed, that's vague.

Now, what to say:

Make an appointment with your professor (rather than use drop-in office hours, unless they are your only choice) and say:

> I'd like to discuss the last exam.

In the professor's office, say:

> I did not do well on the last exam, and I heard you say that most of us didn't do well. Can we look at the part of the test everyone struggled with? Maybe there was an issue with the question? I'm not trying to blame anything or anyone. I would truly like to do better and understand where I'm going wrong. Could you consider letting us make up some of these points?

If you are in the prof's office and you have no idea how the rest of the class did on the exam, you could say,

> Professor, I did very poorly on this exam. Would you be willing to share what the class average was? I would like to know if I was the only one. Maybe I missed something important or didn't fully understand the material as well as I thought I did.

The professor may not share this information, but maybe you can tell by his response. If you can find out about the class average and it is less than 70 percent, you can say,

> I really appreciate you sharing that. It seems like most of us struggled.

(Then you'd continue with a request for the professor to reevaluate the test or let students make up some of the points.)

Your professor may realize the issue himself and decide what to do. Gauge his reaction by watching his body language (if he seems calm or defensive). The professor will likely need time to determine a solution. Again, these situations aren't a quick fix.

The professor may ask you what you expect. You could suggest,

Could we revisit the questions for partial credit?

or

Could we retake a different type of test?

or even

Could you remove those points?

or

Could you grade on a curve?

(Although realize that, if everyone failed, there isn't much of a curve to grade on, is there?)

If the professor is unwilling to do anything about the exam, then you and your classmates will need to take action. Ask tons and tons of questions, request any study tools/guides available, and even ask another professor in the same department for advice on how to improve.

You may even need to ask the dreaded,

Will this be on the test?

to ensure a concrete study base for next time.

Not That:

You sucked at teaching this information, which is why we all failed.

Even if true, blame won't help. Focus on problem solving.

The End Note

I once did horribly on an exam in an anthropology class. I had no idea how the rest of the class was doing. I liked the professor and my other work was going well, but those tests weighted high enough to tank my grade.

At the time, I had taken some education classes, so I had enough beginner knowledge to ask the questions I'm recommending to you. I tentatively approached Professor Anthro (not his real name, of course) and said, "Can we discuss my test grades? I am not sure how the rest of the class is doing, but my scores have been terrible. If you look at my written work, you'll see that I know the material pretty well."

The professor replied, "Things should average out okay for you then."

I shook my head. "The multiple choice tests are weighted pretty high. If you asked me to write a paper about the Yanomamo tribe, I'd do very well."

I didn't know enough to ask about class average. But on final exam day, there was no multiple-choice test! Instead, we watched a film and wrote our interpretation of it.

There was excited buzz in the room as students realized the change. Was I the first to ever challenge Professor Anthro this way? Who knows? But I ended up with a B instead of a C.

If you can nudge a professor to reflect on testing/teaching in general, you've done the professor a huge favor. She may get miffed, but *you have the right to question what doesn't seem correct.* Don't silence yourself because you feel like the underdog. You deserve to respectfully and assertively practice pursuing an issue that concerns you.

You deserve the chance to gain confidence, to become a change agent for yourself and others.

You deserve to find the right words to transform the personal and professional you in incredibly positive ways.

And you deserve to take every single one of those skills with you to use for the rest of your life (and you will!).

There is power in your voice. Use it.

The Career Note

There are times in the workplace when a project goes awry due to lack of proper direction, lack of integral check-ins, etc., on the superior's part. I wondered how learning to self-advocate in college could prepare a student to deal with this situation in the workplace.

> *It's not uncommon for an entire project, team, or even company to fail. When that happens, it's almost always the case that everybody lost contact with the customer. There's an entire "movement" in the startup community around not letting this happen called "Customer Development" which tries to keep startups tethered to reality by getting the team out to see customers often. That approach has two benefits. First, you aren't deluding yourself into thinking everything is okay when it's not, and you can make adjustments. Second, when a problem happens, you've built a rapport with the customer. Most likely they'll be more frank with you, more helpful, and more forgiving—all for what amounts to very little effort. My experience as a student in a major where sometimes the top grade on a test was 50 percent indicates that the same approach works. Being in touch with the reality of your progress in a class means that you aren't trying throw a Hail Mary at the end of the class in the first place. Developing a rapport— making sure the instructor knows your name, that*

you are interested, and working hard—goes a long way towards developing a relationship with the instructor that allows you to ask questions like, "Did everybody blow problem 5 on the test, or was it just me?" When an instructor fails a large portion of the class, they are going to expect a lot of complaints. They will hear from a long line of students who are upset, fearful, angry, and desperate. Their methods, their teaching, and maybe even their motives will be questioned. It's natural for them to become a little defensive. However, if you previously established rapport, your chances of getting answers are much better.

Ted, technology

The Last Note

Congratulations on starting great conversations with your professors and, I bet, breaking out of some of your communication comfort zones!

Two final notes:

First, I welcome your feedback and your questions! If you are dealing with a sticky college situation or you have some thoughts regarding the book, you can message me on *The Chatty Professor* Facebook page, via e-mail at *chattyprof@gmail.com,* or on Twitter *@chattyprof.*

For other communication tips for college success, go to my blog: *http://ellenbremen.com.*

Second, remember that every institution is going to operate differently in terms of policies. Rules and regulations in a two-year college might very well differ from a four-year research institution. However, my guidelines should at least give you a direction to find out what's going on at your school.

Also, as you know, every professor has different perspectives, personalities, etc. This book is based on my opinion and anecdotal evidence from fifteen-plus years of teaching and working with hundreds of students. I am still in the classroom every day. I still experience students every day. However, my experience is just that—my experience. Many colleagues applaud my recommendations, but others may have different views. Still, I invite and encourage you to always start a conversation so you can find out what makes your professor tick.

Finally, I realize that you may read this book because it's assigned to you rather than because you really wanted to. A colleague of mine gave me some harsh truth: "Some students may read the tips and not change one thing." That's very true. There may be absolutely nothing I can say to convince you to alter your communication habits or even talk to a professor in the first place.

But tomorrow—or someday—you may feel completely different. You may encounter a conflict with your professor, or even with someone else in your life, and the tips I've given will suddenly resonate. Then these words will be a change agent for you and the way you are able to conduct yourself. I can't wait to hear about that time when it comes.

Bravo to you for taking steps to become magnificent, assertive communicators. I wish you great abundance on your educational journey.

About the Author

A sixteen-year classroom veteran, Ellen Bremen is tenured faculty in the Communication Studies Department at Highline Community College. Ellen previously taught at Darton College (a two-year unit of the University of Georgia college system), the University of Nevada, Las Vegas, and College of Southern Nevada. Ellen holds degrees in post secondary education and communication. She's also an extremely proud AA degree holder.

As a professor who stops at nothing to help students strengthen their communication skills (think peanut butter and jelly to illustrate problematic messages, pipe cleaners to teach communication models, and Post-it® Notes to reduce speaking anxiety), not surprisingly, Ellen has received awards for teaching innovation from the Sloan Consortium (2011), the National Institute for Staff and Organizational Development, and the National Council of Instructional Administrators (2003). She is a sought-after subject-matter expert in public speaking and interpersonal communication for nearly every single major academic publisher.

Ellen is an advocate for not only students' communication abilities, but also their education as a whole: in 2010–2013, Ellen worked with the Gates Foundation's Open Course Library Grant (in partnership with the Washington State Board of Community and Technical Colleges) when she was competitively selected to serve on the leadership team. This initiative offers open-source 100- and 200-level course materials at a cost of no more than $30 for students, eliminating the need for costly textbooks.

An award-winning public speaker, Ellen also delivers college presentations through Samara Lectures.

You can find Ellen on e-mail via *chattyprof@gmail.com*, on her blog, *The Chatty Professor* (*ellenbremen.com*), on her *Chatty Professor* Facebook page, or on Twitter (*@chattyprof*).

Ellen lives in Seattle, Washington with her husband, Mark, her daughter, Brenna, and her son, Scott.